WHAT'S THE "RIGHT" CAREER?

WHAT'S THE "RIGHT" CAREER?

Useful, Real-Life Advice For High School & College Students From 50+ Professionals

by Tad Berkery

VICARA
BOOKS

Special Sales

Vicara Books are available at a special discount for bulk purchases, for sales promotions and premiums, or for use in corporate training programs. Special editions, including personalized covers, a custom foreword, corporate imprints, and bonus content, are also available.

To Mom and Dad—your unconditional love and support
mean the world to me.

To those working to make the world a kinder place—
thank you for going the extra mile to make an impact.

To everyone reading this dedication—
may this book be a small chapter in your inspiring story.

CONTENTS

7 ENGINEERING

8 ENTREPRENEURSHIP

9 EVENT PLANNING

10 GOVERNMENT, POLITICS, & POLITICAL AFFAIRS

11 HEALTH CARE & MEDICINE

And so the journey begins...

What do you want to be when you grow up? What are you going to major in? What is your passion? What do you want to do with the rest of your life?

Every student has been bombarded with these innocent but deceptively complex questions. I searched for my personal answer to these questions and was unsatisfied with what I found. After scouring the internet, checking out the local bookstore, and asking around, I was troubled to find that there are so few career guidebooks written for students with advice from people actually working in each field of interest. I realized that this represented an opportunity to create a new resource: students all around the country are struggling with these same questions, so why not help everyone to pinpoint their solutions by asking people in various careers about their jobs—what

they like and dislike, how they got there, what advice they would have for those who might want to follow in their footsteps, and what they wish they had known about their industries as a student.

What's the "Right" Career? is composed of detailed responses to a career questionnaire answered by professionals in a range of different fields. These professionals excel at their respective crafts—from individuals who have found their way after making multiple career changes to those who have known what they wanted to do all along. In this book, you will read advice from the chief executive officer of a world leader in women's health, a former special assistant to President Clinton, and a woman who is pioneering the new field of pet rehabilitation, among others. These professionals are sharing their stories and advice to help you craft the career of your dreams.

It is my hope that these insights will empower you to understand what career options are out there and to be active in searching for your passions. Sure, we all know that friend (or maybe you are that person) who is dead set on being a doctor, a political scientist, a writer, etc. But, more realistically, many of us struggle to find our passions or think we know what we want to do but could use some professional advice to make that goal a reality, and that is perfectly okay. Regardless of where you fall on the spectrum of knowing what you want to do, it is worthwhile to understand your options. After all, life is much more fruitful when consumed with an open mind.

So, in the spirit of open-mindedness, enjoy *What's the "Right" Career?* Feel free to read the book cover-to-cover if you are still searching for your passions or skip around directly to specific industries if you think you know your interests. However, regardless of which group you fall into, don't be afraid to dabble in areas that may be new to you, that may be outside the scope of your parents' work, that may be in the arts if you are a steadfast STEM student, or that may be in STEM if you are an arts enthusiast. I think that one of the biggest mistakes we can make as young adults is to naturally get too focused on only what is directly around us, ignoring the vast opportunities that the world has to offer and potentially missing out on the areas in which we may be most talented, most interested, and most able to contribute. You may want to read responses in areas that fall outside your current interests to avoid missing out on an area of interest that you had no idea existed or that may be different than you think. Open your mind to all of the options, and options that you never considered will open their minds to you. And, of course, if you don't know where to start or could use some encouraging words and advice to brighten your day, just flip to a random page and dive into a professional's story ... the best part is that you will learn something new, uplifting, and useful every time.

Looking for a place to start reading?

Below are some particularly memorable lines. Each is included for a particular reason: some because of the great advice that they contain, others for their comical nature, and several that are simply a combination of the two. Some of these lines are original to the respondent; others are mantras quoted from someone else. These lines are highlighted not just to give you good advice or make you laugh but also to give you a sense of what type of person might fit in a given field. If one of these lines makes you laugh, reminds you of yourself, or inspires you to think, take a look at that person's response. You could discover a field that is perfect for you. On the flip side, if you read something and have no idea what it means, check it out. Learning what it means could be the start of identifying a new interest that you never knew you had.

"If you're afraid to admit what you don't know, you'll never learn new things. If you're courageous [enough] to admit your limitations, you'll grow in your strengths."

–See Darien Bates, Page 11

3

"If you are going to dream big, make sure you are surrounded by quality people if you fall."

-See Stefan Muirhead, Page 20

"Managers resolve problems; leaders manage dilemmas."

-See Yvon Brind'Amour, Page 27

"Give me eight weeks and a team of four, and there is no problem that can't be solved."

-See Tim Kuroda, Page 43

"All models are wrong, but some are useful."

-See Seymour Liao, Page 49

"Always choose the path that will teach you the most."

-See Karl Ulrich, Page 75

"Math is not only about things that are useful but about things that are cool."

-See Vern Williams, Page 77

"Never underestimate the need to work well with others. The potential stereotype of techies silently working off in the corner is not true, although there is room for the highly introverted types, with an understanding that advancement will be difficult."

-See Tom Burket, Page 145

"In the 1980s and early '90s, if you had told my mother that I would make a living on the internet, she would have laughed because, at that time, it was not possible."

-See Stefan Muirhead, Page 20

"As a kid, I also spent a lot of time dismantling anything that was held together by a screw to see what was inside—old-style clock radios that had those numbers that would turn over every minute, game machines, watches, toys, portable radios, the lawn mower (Dad was not pleased)—and, to see how tuning worked, I stuck a pair of tweezers into an electrical socket (Dad *really* not pleased)."

-See Viresh Prashar, Page 110

"Coding is a combination of art and science."

-See Ben Paris, Page 53

"Prolific developers don't always write a lot of code; instead they solve a lot of problems. The two things are not the same."

-See Connie Taylor, Page 167

"Unlike other sectors, there is no clear path into government and politics."

-Paul Weinstein, Page 125

"Consulting is a generic term that can mean anything, so, to me, I get to decide my own career path."

-See Steve Tran, Page 45

"Help people do what they love and love what they do."

-See Charlie Choi, Page 129

"If your mother tells you she loves you, check it out."

-See Barb Rehm, Page 175

"If I wasn't getting paid, I'd probably be doing something similar to this anyway."

-See Alan Nash, Page 155

ACKNOWLEDGMENTS

With deep gratitude, I would like to acknowledge the following individuals who helped make *What's the "Right" Career?* a reality by giving thoughtfully and generously with their time, advice, and support ...

Thank you to the thoughtful professionals who donated their time and provided the valuable content that forms the backbone of this book.

Stefan Muirhead and the team at Ignition72— Thank you for helping me think through the delivery of the informational interviews, as well as the structure of the project website, and pointing me to technology and design resources that could support the endeavor.

Rohit Bhargava—Thank you for being a believer in the project as both a professional sharing your story and the publisher of this book.

My parents—With lots of love, thank you for your never-ending patience and support.

1 ADVERTISING, MARKETING, & GRAPHIC DESIGN

DARIEN BATES

FOUNDER AND CHIEF EXECUTIVE OFFICER

DATILEO

Prior Roles: Director, Content Marketing Strategy;
Founding Principal, Creative Strategist;
Account Executive; Staff Reporter.

Education: Bachelor of Arts in Theater,
St. Mary's College of Maryland.

"If you're afraid to admit what you don't know, you'll never learn new things. If you're courageous [enough] to admit your limitations, you'll grow in your strengths."

How did you narrow down your interest(s) to your specific profession?

I made an early effort to take on jobs that were focused on exploration and engagement with a lot of different people in different walks of life. I worked as a reporter for a couple of years learning about what people do and what they are working on. That helped me get a granular sense of what the possibilities were and what really interested me.

When did you first realize that you were interested in your profession? If this occurred during high school, how did you pursue this interest as a high school student?

I knew that I was interested in how people communicate and how those communications reach an audience. In high school, I was very interested in telling stories through writing and theater. However, I didn't really realize that my profession would be in communications until I spent half a year in New York City working with some theater organizations that were doing great work but weren't able to communicate their message and mission effectively.

I realized that just doing great work wasn't enough. It was necessary to focus on communicating that work out to a wider audience.

It became a focus for me then, and has remained one, as I've explored the different techniques and technologies that can broaden the reach of organizations doing good work.

How did you break into the industry associated with your profession? What advice would you have for a high school student who is interested in breaking into the same industry?

I was lucky in meeting people who took a chance on someone who had little experience but a lot of energy and commitment.

I would recommend that young people take every opportunity available to try new things. It doesn't always have to look exactly like what you want to do, but, if you commit to doing it fully, people will remember you for that, and you may find natural pathways open up to what you want to do.

What advice would you have for high school students who are interested in a profession that is similar to yours? Is there anything specific you suggest that these high school students should do?

The world of communications and marketing is pretty tight-knit. People will remember you. If you leave a positive impression, your world will grow in opportunities. If you leave negative impressions, your opportunities will dwindle.

What are some aspects of your profession that the average high school student would not know but should know? What are some aspects that surprise you about your profession?

Regardless of your area of focus in marketing/communications, it's increasingly important to understand data and statistics. Behind all the creativity of marketing is a lot of data.

I didn't realize that at first, and now I find that a large part of what I do is work with data to support creative communications.

If you were to hire the ideal job candidate for your profession, what kind of person would you be hiring? What qualities would this person have?

I always look for people who are fascinated with learning new things and generous with applying what they know, while acknowledging what they don't. The world is changing very quickly, and it's impossible to know everything. Being open to learning new things is essential to remaining relevant, and being open to one's own limitations gives others the opportunity to contribute and understand how to collaborate effectively.

What are your favorite and least-favorite parts about your profession?

Favorite—The opportunity to work with a lot of different organizations to solve challenges that, when solved, have measurable benefits to a lot of people.

Least-favorite—Negotiating contracts. I sometimes wish we could deliver what we do to everyone, regardless of ability to pay. However, ensuring profitability is also an essential discipline in business, and it does provide an important source of feedback that shapes what we do according to what people are willing to "buy."

STEPHANIE KURODA

CHIEF MARKETING OFFICER

INTRAFI NETWORK

Prior Roles: *VP, Marketing at Collaborex; Director of Strategy & Marketing at Howrey; Marketing Manager at General Mills; Assistant Vice President at Bank of Boston.*

Education: *BA Economics, Wellesley College; MBA, Harvard Business School.*

"It's not about you; it's about them."

How did you narrow down your interest(s) to your specific profession?

For me, it was a process—a process that was years in the making and that involved trial and error and the combining of skills and interests I learned from "trying out" different roles.

To start, after graduating from college, I went into commercial lending. I was hired by a large regional bank that had a formal loan officer training program for new hires. Thanks to that program and on-the-job learning under the wings of vice presidents and assistant vice presidents who served as mentors, I learned how to analyze financial statements, to model future cash flows under base-case, best-case, and worst-case scenarios, and to present a proposed loan to a credit committee both orally and in writing.

I liked what I did very much, but I also learned an important thing that turned me off to that field on a long-term basis—mainly that successful lenders became more and more responsible for selling as they moved up the corporate ladder. That did not mesh well with my personality; I am an introvert who prefers to work behind the scenes rather than on the frontline.

So, while still working as a corporate lender, I quietly applied for several advertising positions. Unfortunately, I was not able to land an interview. I looked like a career changer with no background to leverage. And that is what I was.

13

So off to business school I went—to gain exposure to additional fields (e.g., marketing, operations, organizational behavior, etc.) and the credibility I thought I needed to open the door to a wider array of career options.

In business school, I took a detailed personality test—one with hundreds of questions (bubbles) to fill with a No. 2 pencil. The assessment indicated that I had high interests in analytical and creative areas and suggested that I pursue those kinds of roles. Interestingly, a counselor told me that I would probably have to pick one of these two areas to focus on for my career and to get my "fix" in the other area through hobbies.

That knowledge pointed me in a more defined set of directions. The business school I attended helped to open doors, and an internship in consumer product marketing helped me to try out this field of interest to confirm that what I thought I wanted to do was indeed a decent choice for me.

I was fortunate in that I was able to garner a job in marketing. Initially, I worked in brand management combining both art (e.g., leading the development of storyboards for ads and videos, the selection of package designs, etc.) and science (e.g., calculating break-evens; analyzing sensitivities; and monitoring overall sales volume, shelf facings, distribution, coupon redemptions, and promotional trade-offs). Eventually, I moved into business-to-business marketing and then into related strategy roles. All of this led up to where I am today, working on strategy and implementation and both business-to-business and business-to-consumer marketing. I like where I am now, having stayed in the field for decades now, but who knows? I may have another career in me when I get closer to retirement age.

When did you first realize that you were interested in your profession? If this occurred during high school, how did you pursue this interest as a high school student?

I did not know in high school—or college or even in the early part of my career—what I wanted to do. Some people know very early on. Not me. No way. No, siree.

Personally, I think it's difficult to determine which careers to explore when you're young because you are still growing into yourself, figuring out who you are and what's important to you, and most likely have not had a substantive chance to try out different work-oriented roles to see what they're actually like.

The good news is that it's okay if you don't know what you want to do. Lots of people don't know and figure it out as they go.

How did you break into the industry associated with your profession? What advice would you have for a high school student who is interested in breaking into the same industry?

I broke into marketing by seeking out a brand management internship with a well-known manufacturer of consumer package goods. I was fortunate enough not only to get such an internship, but to get one with an industry leader (which provided "street cred" and made the experience look more transferrable to competitors and others). I was also lucky enough to be able to prove myself in the role and to receive an offer for more permanent employment.

I actually had a blast working as an intern; work seems less like work when you like what you do and are surrounded by people you like. (Mind you, as one of my former roommates put it: work is still work. If it's not hard or difficult, everyone would want to do it for the fun of it and you wouldn't get paid.)

What are some aspects of your profession that the average high school student would not know but should know? What are some aspects that surprise you about your profession?

In my humble opinion, the key is to learn "base" skills, like how to communicate, how to figure things out, how to prioritize, and how to manage your time.

These are the skills to learn in high school (and college and afterwards). These are the skills you'll apply on the job, no matter what field or industry you end up in. These are the skills you'll be able to bring to different roles. These are the skills that will provide you with the flexibility and confidence to try something new (some new field, some new job experience) and then to pursue it further.

Another thing to do is to explore. Try new things to see if anything catches your fancy. For example:

- Ask people (e.g., your parents, your parents' friends, your friends' parents) about what they do for a living.
- Network; ask friends, friends of friends, and extended family for informational interviews and/or the ability to shadow people in their jobs for a day (perhaps for Bring Your Sons and Daughters to Work Day, even if you are not literally the son or daughter of the employee in question, as workplaces often organize special activities for that day).
- Look for internships, volunteer to work on projects in your field of interest, or create your own project (as the Editor of *What's the "Right" Career?* has done). Summer break is a great time for this…. Then, keep "rinsing and repeating" until you find something you love.

You may not strike gold with your first undertaking, but that's okay because figuring out what you don't want to do is valuable learning as well.

And you might find that one role, even if it's not the "right role" for you, opens the door to a different, better one.

What are some aspects of your profession that the average high school student would not know but should know? What are some aspects that surprise you about your profession?

As you move up, you spend more and more time managing people—that is, on organizational behavior, human resources, and policy-related issues—which leaves a lot less time available to focus on pure marketing.

Also, most companies are not marketing-driven companies. Most companies are sales- or technology-driven, leaving marketing more in a support role and more vulnerable to expense-cutting.

If you were to hire the ideal job candidate for your profession, what kind of person would you be hiring? What qualities would this person have?

What I look for varies by position and level, but, generally, I'm looking for someone who can think and who can communicate, as well as someone who will fit with the company's culture. Someone who can think will learn quickly on the job in general and as the market evolves. Someone who can communicate can not only create persuasive marketing materials, but also sell an idea internally (across functions and up the management chain). Someone who fits in will have more fun at work and be more fun to work with.

What are your favorite and least-favorite parts about your profession?

My three favorite things about marketing:

1. It blends art and science.
2. It brings together strategy and implementation.
3. I never get tired of what I do. There's always a new challenge: changing tastes and technological advancements mean it's forever evolving.

My three least-favorite things about marketing:

1. Everybody thinks they know marketing.
2. People tend to think about their own experiences and what they like or would do. This natural tendency is often difficult to combat. With marketing, however, one has to get beyond that to recognize that it's not about what you want or what you would do; it's actually about what the customer wants and what the customer would do. Frequently, your profile isn't going to match a target customer's persona, meaning you have to at least temporarily put yourself in a different mindset—the customer's mindset.
3. Marketing involves crafting a focused message, but, often, the people involved in crafting that message embrace the kitchen sink in an effort to please various (dare I say "all"?) internal parties involved in the development process. The answer to the question "What is the one (or first) thing you want a customer to know?" shouldn't be everything under the sun. That's too much to communicate in a headline, and attention spans run short.

AMY MANSHIP

DIRECTOR OF MARKETING

INTRAFI NETWORK

Prior Roles: *Graphic Designer, Senior Graphic Designer, Creative Director, Marketing Director.*

Education: *Bachelor's Degree in Art from the University of Alabama in Huntsville.*

"Work hard, do your best, continually think of solutions. Everything is a puzzle to be solved. Find inspiration wherever you can."

How did you narrow down your interest(s) to your specific profession?

I have always liked art and drawing. My mom was always having me take some art or craft class growing up. I took fine arts as an elective my sophomore and junior years of high school but was on an engineering track as far as the rest of my classes were concerned. The summer before my senior year, I was selected to represent my

high school in an eight-week summer job program with NASA. I worked in a propulsion lab and wrote a paper about my time there. There were probably twenty of us at different job sites from high schools all around Huntsville, Alabama. I hated it. Probably not the conclusion the program intended, but it moved me away from engineering as a career. So in my senior year of high school, I dropped AP Calculus and picked up graphic design/photography.

When did you first realize that you were interested in your profession? If this occurred during high school, how did you pursue this interest as a high school student?

The graphic design/photography class I took in high school showed me the career possibilities of art as a career. I could get a job and not just be a starving artist. It was a great revelation to me to know that I could work in a creative field and get paid.

How did you break into the industry associated with your profession? What advice would you have for a high school student who is interested in breaking into the same industry?

I worked really hard and volunteered for anything in the Art Department that might let me learn. In college, our Art Department did not have a computer lab for the graphic design classes yet; it was 1989. We still had to do our designs with markers, paint, and hand lettering. Then the department got two computers. Just two. One of our assignments was to take a major brand and recreate a new brand for it: to go through a redesign and a complete style guide. Hand-drawn. They asked for two volunteers to take the style manuals and put them in the design software on the computers—to learn the program and then put each of the student's style manuals in Adobe PageMaker on the computer. There was no pay, only the perk of learning the two programs they had—FreeHand and PageMaker. I was one of the volunteers. Learning the programs got me a couple of other department assignments, and it also got me selected for an internship with the local newspaper's art department. And, when I graduated, an actual job with the same newspaper's art department.

What advice would you have for high school students who are interested in a profession that is similar to yours? Is there anything specific that you suggest that these high school students should do?

With art, it is practice. And not just creating on the computer. It is learning the basics: how colors work together, how creating with different mediums feels.

It is continuing to learn and love your craft and get better—taking classes, learning from people/ teachers who have experience with it. There are many, many more classes in school now to explore jobs in art. Mine ultimately ended up being in marketing. Find an application of what you love (jobs) so that you can make a living.

What are some aspects of your profession that the average high school student would not know but should know? What are some aspects that surprise you about your profession?

Even with creative work, like art, the business part of work is important, too. How to explain why you choose the design, the color, the image, the words (yes, artists need to be able to write words, too) is extremely important. As an artist, you must sell your idea to the client; you must sell the thought, the vision, the reasoning behind the creative to your boss, to your CEO. And there has to be a point to what you do with graphic design besides the fact that it is pretty. Communication is as important as the creative: communication to the audience, whether that be your boss to get it approved or the end customer who would purchase whatever it is.

If you were to hire the ideal job candidate for your profession, what kind of person would you be hiring? What qualities would this person have?

That depends. Entry-level designer—talent, intelligence, willingness to work, willingness to learn, general personality fit with the rest of the team. A more experienced designer—talent, intelligence, willingness to work, willingness to learn, personality fit, *plus* understanding of the product, the ability to think strategically about what we do and apply that to their work.

Please provide a quote or mantra that you feel accurately reflects both you and your profession. It can be a quote generated by you or a quote from someone else. If the quote or mantra is from someone else, please specify who generated the quote or mantra.

Work hard, do your best, and continually think of solutions. Everything is a puzzle to be solved. Find inspiration wherever you can.

Please list your favorite three aspects of your profession.

1. Marketing and design is about problem-solving, and I love trying to figure out the best way to make someone understand what I am trying to explain.

2. Getting to start with a blank page and create something from nothing. This was one of my drivers to go into design. The thought of doing the same job every day for the rest of my life was terrifying to me in high school.

3. Working in a group of creative people.

Please list your three least-favorite aspects about your profession.

I don't have a lot of knocks on my profession; I like it. I like going to work every day. But I will list some things that are not from my current job but about my profession in general …

1. Sometimes there are people that are hard to work with; not all creative people are also collaborative.

2. Sometimes no matter how you try, your idea will not fly, will not get approved, and/or will change from your concept to an unrecognizable end. Art professions require compromise and thick skin. It's not a bad thing, just is.

That is it, that's all I have …

Additional Comments:

Figuring out what you want to do for a career is hard. And not everybody hits it out of the ballpark the first time. Many people have two or three careers in their lifetime. I was lucky in that I kind of knew art was what I wanted to do. I just had to figure out how to monetize it so that I could support myself and be independent. Check out the things you love to see what application there is for a career. Work hard. Seek opportunities to learn. Be able to speak about yourself, your abilities, your work. Good luck!

STEFAN MUIRHEAD

FOUNDER AND MANAGING PARTNER (STRATEGY)

IGNITION72 [DIGITAL MARKETING AGENCY]

Education: *I have a Bachelor of Arts degree from the University of Glasgow, with a focus on classic subjects: Languages, History, Roman Government, Philosophy, and Economics.*

"Loyalty above all else, except honor."

"Utility is seven-eighths proximity."

— *Iain M. Banks*
(Science-Fiction Author)

How did you narrow down your interest(s) to your specific profession?

My dad worked in corporate marketing and sales, and I got to go along with him to some advertising agency meetings in the late '80s and early '90s. This turned into some internships and then to real relationships, which helped me get a job right out of college. I wanted to work in advertising for two reasons. First, because it is fun. Second, most jobs have you doing the same thing for the same people day in and day out. But in advertising, you might work on four different clients' projects in one day. You never know what you will be working on. Meanwhile, there is a lot of variety and a ton of interesting, bright, creative people. For one of my first job interviews I was asked why I wanted to be in advertising. I answered that I want to change the world, but I do not want to be a politician. Today advertising is better characterized as communications, and it is everywhere you look.

When did you first realize that you were interested in your profession? If this occurred during high school, how did you pursue this interest as a high school student?

I knew that I wanted to be in advertising when I was twelve. I was not very popular at school. I was a nerd who was not that athletic. During the summer of my sophomore and junior years, I got internships at a couple of agencies. At these agencies, people appreciated my wit and my intelligence. Nobody beat me up. Honestly, I fit, and I knew it, and so did the people I was working with.

The best advice to getting a job in advertising that I received was simple: live an interesting life, communicate well, know how to write, and be willing to serve others and their goals. The great thing about what I do is that my style is all me; it's not what school I went to or a specific training program I was in.

In communications you get to be yourself on some level, which is both scary and freeing. So as a high school student, I was myself—learning, exploring, taking it all in. I found some teachers and other adults whom I could talk to. They were willing to help me think through complex concepts, act as advisors, and help me get where I wanted to be.

How did you break into the industry associated with your profession? What advice would you have for a high school student who is interested in breaking into the same industry?

At the top of the game, I would say get an internship. Learning from others is always the best way, and you create relationships that can last a lifetime and be of great use. That having been said, sometimes you cannot work for free (most internships are not,

or badly, paid). If that is the case, hit the internet for online courses, books, videos, and anything else that the professionals are using. Figure out if the industry you like has lots of acronyms (if it does, learn them). Understand the career path that industry has to offer. See if there is a public forum online, a subreddit, or other place where people are talking about it. You want to fill your head with as much about that career industry as you can so you have something to talk about during interviews. Everybody is asked "Why do you want to do X?" "Because I need a paycheck" is a bad answer. Having a great answer will set you apart.

What advice would you have for high school students who are interested in a profession that is similar to yours? Is there anything specific that you suggest that these high school students should do?

My world has become very technology-focused, and high school students tend to be good users of technology. If I were talking to high schoolers, I would encourage them to go beyond just using technology. Also, explore creating technology, measuring technology, documenting technology, and training others on how to use technology. Technology is an industry; there are so many subcategories that anybody and everybody could work in technology. Also, learn to type and write. If you cannot type thirty-five words per-minute, you are slow. If you can write well, you can always find a job as a communicator.

What are some aspects of your profession that the average high school student would not know but should know? What are some aspects that surprise you about your profession?

Personal relationships are critical in what I do for a living. Being a nice guy, up to speed on the latest news stories, and able to converse about a wide range of topics is critical in what I do as a new businessperson.

However, I am not just a new businessperson. I am also an owner of a company, and the role I play with regard to that is a little harder to pin down.

In any organization, there are dedicated people who are the voice of the organization, the brains of the organization, or the arms and legs of the organization. But somebody has to be the heart.

How does the company treat people, engage clients, address problems, and celebrate victories? How does the company want to be treated? This comes from every employee, but it starts at the top. In short, all of those things every mom worries about matter. They are almost addressed automatically when you are polite, friendly, honest, hardworking, well-dressed, etc. Take those things and add a saleable skill, and you will be successful. Ignore them, and the path is not impossible; it is just much less efficient because fewer doors open on their own.

If you were to hire the ideal job candidate for your profession, what kind of person would you be hiring? What qualities would this person have?

We are always looking for the right personality with some of the right skills. We never hire the perfect skills with a so-so personality.

After running the company for many years, we see a common trend—people who leave do so because of fit and personality, not because of capability (we have a number of employees who have been here almost a decade). At our company, we are small, so everybody being on the same page and seeing eye to eye is critical. That is why when we interview new staff, we let all employees participate and have a say. Apart from personality,

the things from the previous question all count, too. We ask ourselves whether a person wants to be and is capable of being a part of our team and representing our company, as well as able to grow, learn, and improve. We do not let preconceptions get in the way. By the way, our creative director was hired from Best Buy, and our star programmer worked at Rite Aid before joining our company. These are incredibly talented people who just needed somebody to give them a chance to reach their potential.

Please provide a quote or mantra that you feel accurately reflects both you and your profession.

"Utility is seven-eighths proximity." —Iain M. Banks, Sci-Fi Author. Basically acknowledging that the best solution is the one close at hand.

"Loyalty above all else, except honor." This is my personal mantra that I have been using since I was a kid. I believe the Marines use it as well. It has been around since Roman times and does not have an author.

Please list your favorite three aspects of your profession.

1. The rapidly changing, always-evolving tech space. The tech space does not stop, even when you want it to. There is always something new to learn, test, and try.

2. Even though we work with technology, at the end of the day we work for people. We build things that people use, and people are the center of everything that we do. We are a people company!

3. The people I get to work with are great. My father works at my company, as does my best friend of twenty years. I trust the team, and know they have my back, just as I have theirs.

This is more to do with my current job than my profession.

Please list your three least-favorite aspects about your profession.

1. Money. As a small business, everything comes down to money (got to pay the bills), and factoring that in is something that I dislike. Sometimes you cannot do what you want to do or what you know is right, simply because of a lack of funds.

2. Rapid change. Yes, I list this as a plus as well, but it is also a negative. Sometimes I wish the world would just stand still a little while so I could catch up!

3. The lack of standardization, accountability, or tried-and-true approaches. Given that my industry is fairly new (twenty years tops), there are nowhere near the established and accepted processes that other industries enjoy. This is an opportunity, but it also means that you are often wading through uncharted territory.

How has your industry changed since the pandemic?

They say that situations like these only accelerate what was already happening, and we see that truth in the interactive space right now. The internet is more important than before, so business is up; but everybody is working remotely, which introduces new challenges, not only in getting things done, but also in doing them efficiently.

At the moment, the greatest thing about our career path specifically is that we have the opportunity to help great clients weather this storm. Our cities' school district, housing authority, and numerous other clients are all working to help people in need, and it is a wonderful thing to be able to help them.

This situation is forcing us to evolve even faster. We must be able to efficiently communicate, which means using dozens of different programs (basically anything our clients use). We no longer have the automatic privilege of in-person meetings and user testing, but the work still has to be done.

On top of that, we have to figure out what to do with a 7,000-square-foot office that we rent for a fair amount of money per month, and which now only ever holds two to three people at any one time.

Additional Comments:

More than before, the landscape of business is being redefined way more than I would have predicted. This is, in my opinion, because of technology; it pervades every facet of our lives.

I think that young people who are daunted by their possible futures should not be afraid to explore alternative paths. This can include starting your own company, working flex hours, or remotely, or having multiple part-time jobs. I do not think there is clarity on what the "right" path forward is (when I was a kid, there were much fewer options).

In the 1980s and early '90s, if you had told my mother that I would make a living on the internet, she would have laughed because, at that time, it was not possible.

Another key point: if you are going to dream big, make sure you are surrounded by quality people if you fall. These are your family, your friends, your teammates, and they all play a role in your career.

2 BANKING, FINANCE, & FINANCIAL SERVICES

See the following interviews that relate to Banking, Finance, & Financial Services:

Chris Kraft, Page 152

YVON BRIND'AMOUR

FORMER CHIEF FINANCIAL OFFICER

LAFARGE NORTH AMERICA

Prior Roles: Financial Analyst, Controller (Division), VP Finance (Division), VP Investor Relations (Corporate).

Education: Baccalaureate Degree in Business Administration; Baccalaureate Degree in Accounting; Professional Certification.

"Managers resolve problems; leaders manage dilemmas (i.e., complex, chaotic problems which might not have a perfect 'solution')."

How did you narrow down your interest(s) to your specific profession?

Trial and error! With time, I decided to concentrate on the finance/accounting field instead of HR management (my original first choice).

When did you first realize that you were interested in your profession? If this occurred during high school, how did you pursue this interest as a high school student?

It happened AFTER I graduated. I took ten years of night courses to obtain my professional designation.

How did you break into the industry associated with your profession? What advice would you have for a high school student who is interested in breaking into the same industry?

In my profession, the industry is not the main factor; the finance jobs are easily "transportable" from one industry to another.

What advice would you have for high school students who are interested in a profession that is similar to yours? Is there anything specific that you suggest that these high school students should do?

If interested in business administration-related professions, one should take as many math-related subjects as possible.

Because the professional will eventually have to manage people, psychology courses are also essential (in fact, social sciences represent a very good complement to math!).

What are some aspects of your profession that the average high school student would not know but should know? What are some aspects that surprise you about your profession?

Managing people in order to get their full attention, dedication, and power.

Very often, students in business or engineering focus on the "core" math or science subjects. But sooner or later, you have to interact with PEOPLE to get leverage for your ideas.

If you were to hire the ideal job candidate for your profession, what kind of person would you be hiring? What qualities would this person have?

In addition to having the basic skills (as demonstrated by a degree or belonging to a professional association—CPA in this case), I am looking for flexibility, open-mindedness, and interpersonal skills (i.e., natural leadership attributes).

Please list your favorite three aspects of your profession.

Business meetings / teamwork (problem resolution as a team). Project management (i.e., buying and selling businesses, mergers, etc.). Developing people and seeing them grow in life.

Please list your three least-favorite aspects about your profession.

The "dry" side of accounting: producing reports, basic analyses, etc. Managing downturns: making the difficult "people-related" decisions.

How has your industry changed since the pandemic?

As far as I am concerned, COVID did not change much for me ... except that my tennis season has been hampered!

Since working at Lafarge North America as chief financial officer, I have started teaching. I have converted my five courses so that I may give them online. We use VIA (a competitor of Zoom, but more for "professional" use) for the courses, to which I have added PowerPoints with comments for review between courses.

It was a bit of work, learning the tool (enough to be perfectly at ease with it), converting all the materials so it is possible to convey the subjects seamlessly, and modifying the exams since all documents will be available for the students.

The investment was well worth it since I give two courses this summer, and three in the fall (we've already decided that they will be online this fall as well!), all in the comfort of my home.

MILITARY MEDICINE REGIONAL COMPTROLLER

DEPARTMENT OF DEFENSE

Prior Roles: *Supervisory Financial Management Analyst, Financial Management Analyst, Budget Analyst.*

Education: *California State University, Northridge City University, Defense Acquisition University.*

"The mission comes first!"

How did you narrow down your interest(s) to your specific profession?

Jobs held earlier in my career led me to this career field. I did not choose it at first; I "fell into" the financial field.

When did you first realize that you were interested in your profession? If this occurred during high school, how did you pursue this interest as a high school student?

Once in the financial field, I found that this was my forte. I love analysis, creating spreadsheets, tracking, doing my part to help meet the mission.

How did you break into the industry associated with your profession? What advice would you have for a high school student who is interested in breaking into the same industry?

I started out with lower-grade positions and worked my way up by building a foundation of knowledge and experience.

My advice is to study mathematics, business, and finance. If you are not a logical, analytical person, this is not the right field for you.

What advice would you have for high school students who are interested in a profession that is similar to yours? Is there anything specific that you suggest that these high school students should do?

Study mathematics, business, and finance in school. As mentioned above, if you are not a logical, analytical person, this is not the right field for you.

Don't try to start at the top; you must first build a foundation of knowledge and experience to be successful (in addition to obtaining the right college degree).

What are some aspects of your profession that the average high school student would not know but should know? What are some aspects that surprise you about your profession?

I am not always in control of my day. You must be able to multi-task and prioritize work. You start the day with a plan of what you want to accomplish, but higher-priority, "hot" issues always come up that require immediate attention.

If you were to hire the ideal job candidate for your profession, what kind of person would you be hiring? What qualities would this person have?

The ideal candidate would have great logical and analytical skills, have a forte for finance, be a team player, and also able to work well independently. The ideal candidate would love working in the financial field.

Please list your favorite three aspects of your profession.

1. Ever-changing priorities to keep me on my toes!
2. Always new issues/problems to solve.
3. Great job satisfaction (due to being a part of a great mission).

Please list your three least-favorite aspects about your profession.

1. Ever-changing priorities (!).
2. Always new issues/problems to solve (!).
3. My day is not necessarily my own.

How has your industry changed since the pandemic?

During the COVID-19 pandemic, for our safety and the safety of the community, the majority of our employees were sent home to telework until such time as it is deemed to be safe for us to return to our regular worksites.

After nearly three months of teleworking, I really miss being able to walk out of my office and discuss things with my team and the other folks in the building. I miss being able to ask questions and get immediate answers. I miss attending meetings in person and being able to read people's "body language."

Teleworking has its advantages, but I'm definitely feeling the disadvantages. I'm ready to go back to work outside of my dining room "office." I do, however, want to stay safe and healthy, want to keep my family and community safe and healthy, and I understand the need to stay at home.

Until the order is given to return, I shall continue to give 200 percent effort from the comfort and safety of my home.

Additional Comments:

Working for the federal government is great! Working in the financial field is great!

ANN EPSTEIN

DIRECTOR OF PROJECT MANAGEMENT

FREDDIE MAC

Prior Roles: *I have held a variety of roles related to product management, product marketing, project management, business process redesign, and change management. I have had a number of roles within Freddie Mac that provided a good understanding of the mortgage market.*

Education: *Bachelor of Science in Economics (Finance Major) and Bachelor of Applied Science (Systems Engineering Major)—University of Pennsylvania; Master in Business Administration—The Wharton School.*

Note: Ann Epstein would like readers to know that this contribution is solely her own and not a position or contribution provided or endorsed by Freddie Mac.

How did you narrow down your interest(s) to your specific profession?

Mostly through discovering what aspects of roles I liked and didn't like during my career. For example, I liked the problem-solving and project orientation of consulting, but I didn't like the travel or the selling aspects, so I found internal roles that were projects that drove change without the selling or travel. Within that, I liked shaping and introducing a product to market more than I liked projects associated with business transformational changes.

When did you first realize that you were interested in your profession? If this occurred during high school, how did you pursue this interest as a high school student?

I didn't know that product management existed as a career in high school. It wasn't until graduate school that I started to gravitate toward it, and it was not really until several years after that that I decided it was an area I wanted to focus on.

How did you break into the industry associated with your profession? What advice would you have for a high school student who is interested in breaking into the same industry?

The industry I am in is financial services and, specifically, mortgage finance. Most of the people interested in financial services major in business, but the reality is we are a data and technology company as much as anything else. The products we bring to market are financial products, but they are backed by data and technology.

Majoring in business is one option, but data sciences or information technology are also good options. There are good training programs in financial institutions that are good ways to start to learn the industry, and consulting is also a good option.

What advice would you have for high school students who are interested in a profession that is similar to yours? Is there anything specific that you suggest that these high school students should do?

No matter what you major in, you also need to focus on your communication skills (both listening, as well as spoken and written communication), your project management and organizational skills, and your interpersonal and relationship-management skills. Those are just as important as specific technical knowledge.

What are some aspects of your profession that the average high school student would not know but should know? What are some aspects that surprise you about your profession?

The world of finance is changing so rapidly that by the time you graduate from college, it will be a very different world. Paper mortgages will be a thing of the past soon, computer programs will do more and more of the tasks associated with the transactions, and blockchains may replace much of the role of financial institutions.

If you were to hire the ideal job candidate for your profession, what kind of person would you be hiring? What qualities would this person have?

I tend to hire people with industry knowledge who have been successful project managers on business projects. I look for good communication skills and fast learners.

Please list your favorite three aspects of your profession.

- Constantly changing/constantly learning new things.
- Satisfaction when something you envisioned is finally brought to life and it's successful.
- Working with customers for successful outcome.

Please list your three least-favorite aspects about your profession.

Politics / bureaucracy. Deadlines / stress / sometimes long hours. Not all projects are successful; sometimes you work hard on something and the project is killed before it hits the market, or the change doesn't match the business case and you have to kill it soon after. Sometimes projects implement very late or customers don't like the product, etc.

How has your industry changed since the pandemic?

From an immediate perspective, corporately our focus has shifted toward providing liquidity to the housing market. The focus is on: (1) providing forbearance and loss mitigation options for homeowners who may have been impacted by the crisis, and (2) maintaining liquidity for lenders so they can continue to make loans during the crisis. Making loans during a pandemic has some interesting barriers, including navigating the current parts of the process that require in-person contact. It is personally gratifying to me that earlier in my career at Freddie Mac I was responsible for creating the policy and building infrastructure to enable electronic mortgages (a digitally signed asset). Adoption of eMortgages had been very slow for many years, but now that it is needed during this crisis, it is available to lenders. The pandemic has shifted the mortgage market overnight from purchase to refinance and from getting people into homes to keeping people in their homes. It is good to feel like we are doing our part.

TERRENCE MANNING

CERTIFIED PUBLIC ACCOUNTANT (CPA)

FINANCE AND ACCOUNTING PROFESSIONAL WITH
PUBLICLY TRADED AND PRIVATE COMPANY EXPERIENCE

Prior Roles: *Various roles of increasing responsibility in finance, accounting, and operations. Began career as auditor with a "Big 6" accounting firm (now "Big 4").*

Education: *Bachelor of Science in Accountancy (BSA), Villanova University; Master of Business Administration (MBA), Finance Concentration, St. Joseph's University.*

"The right thing is not always easy, and the easy thing is not always right."

How did you narrow down your interest(s) to your specific profession?

I enjoyed my accounting class in high school, and I had an older sister who was graduating college with an accounting degree and who had landed a good job out of college, so I knew it was a profession that, if you worked hard, could land you a good job upon graduation.

When did you first realize that you were interested in your profession? If this occurred during high school, how did you pursue this interest as a high school student?

I took an accounting class in high school and enjoyed it and the business aspect of it, so when I applied to college, I focused on colleges with strong business programs.

How did you break into the industry associated with your profession? What advice would you have for a high school student who is interested in breaking into the same industry?

I did a college internship with a small accounting firm during my junior year of college, but nothing accounting-related prior to that. It's sometimes difficult to break into an industry while you are still in high school or are early in your college years, so I would recommend seeking out people in industries of interest and asking them for advice and the path they took in getting in the industry.

What advice would you have for high school students who are interested in a profession that is similar to yours? Is there anything specific that you suggest that these high school students should do?

Although there is obviously a component of accounting that is math/computational, I would recommend that students work at improving their communication skills, both written and verbal.

What are some aspects of your profession that the average high school student would not know but should know? What are some aspects that surprise you about your profession?

One thing that I think surprises people is that accounting is not just a "numbers" thing. There

is quite a lot of interaction with people, quite a lot of writing involved. So one's written and verbal communication skills are extremely important.

If you were to hire the ideal job candidate for your profession, what kind of person would you be hiring? What qualities would this person have?

Ethical, hardworking, and inquisitive with good communication skills, and a willingness to continue to seek improvement.

What are your favorite and least-favorite parts about your profession?

Change can often be a least favorite, at least at first, but it does add variety to the job, which is a plus. Favorite part is dealing with and interacting with people, whether they be coworkers, vendors, or clients.

3 BEAUTY & PERSONAL CARE

Monica Mather
OWNER AND STYLIST

MONICA MATHER

OWNER AND STYLIST

SALON FLEUR DE LIS

Prior Roles: *Hairstylist, Salon Manager.*

Education: *Cosmetology School, three years of college at George Mason University.*

"If you don't have a passion for the art and business of hairdressing, then you're just cutting hair."
— Tabatha Coffey

How did you narrow down your interest(s) to your specific profession?

I have always been interested in hair and fashion. I knew from a very early age that my life plan would involve becoming a hairstylist. I decided to jump into owning a small business because my profits would increase and give me independence.

When did you first realize that you were interested in your profession? If this occurred during high school, how did you pursue this interest as a high school student?

I was about five years old when my mom started to notice that I would only color in the hair of the pictures in all my coloring books. When asked as a child what I wanted to be when I grew up, I always said I wanted to be a hairstylist.

How did you break into the industry associated with your profession? What advice would you have for a high school student who is interested in breaking into the same industry?

I started working in hair salons at the age of sixteen. I worked in reception and as a shampooer until I was able to be more hands-on and then became an assistant. This was great for me because I saw how hard stylists worked and got to experience every position in a hair salon.

What advice would you have for high school students who are interested in a profession that is similar to yours? Is there anything specific that you suggest that these high school students should do?

I would suggest that they get a job working at a hair salon. They would see the pace that salons work at and whether or not they would enjoy the job. Many think that it's a glamorous job, but in truth it is messy and exhausting.

You truly have to be passionate about what you do in order to be successful in this industry.

What are some aspects of your profession that the average high school student would not know but should know? What are some aspects that surprise you about your profession?

As mentioned above, the fact that it's not glamorous. It is hard on your body, your feet, and back especially.

Also, it requires extensive continuing education. It can be very profitable, but your income directly reflects how much and how hard you work.

If you were to hire the ideal job candidate for your profession, what kind of person would you be hiring? What qualities would this person have?

Someone very personable and professional with the desire and ability to make people feel good and with a strong sense of style. I would also want someone who is willing to work hard and always continue learning, someone passionate.

Please list your favorite three aspects of your profession.

1. Connecting with people on a deep and personal level.
2. No two days are ever the same. You get to create and be trusted by your clients with the only accessory they will wear every day.
3. The opportunity for growth is always available to those who want it.

Please list your three least-favorite aspects about your profession.

1. It can be absolutely exhausting!
2. You need to be able to work when people are off (nights, weekends, and holidays sometimes!).
3. Sometimes people can see you as a commodity and not a person.

4 CONSULTING

TIM KURODA

PRINCIPAL

GLOBAL CONSULTING FIRM

Prior Roles: *Managing Director, Director, Manager, Senior Associate.*

Education: *BA Political Science, Yale University; MBA Management, Stern School of Business at New York University.*

"Give me eight weeks and a team of four, and there is no problem that can't be solved."

How did you narrow down your interest(s) to your specific profession?

I spoke to people in the consulting industry, as well as other fields that I thought might be a good fit for me (e.g., investment banking, corporate law). Through those discussions, I felt consulting was the best match for my skills and interests.

When did you first realize that you were interested in your profession? If this occurred during high school, how did you pursue this interest as a high school student?

Senior year of college.

How did you break into the industry associated with your profession? What advice would you have for a high school student who is interested in breaking into the same industry?

I got my first opportunity as a full-time hire after I graduated from college. I went through the formal recruiting process during the spring of my senior year of college.

For high school students, I would focus on developing skills, rather than focusing on a specific set of classes. The skills and tools to develop would include effective writing, oral presentation, having a broad vocabulary, mathematics and statistics, graphical representation, and analytics. Developing a baseline understanding of business, finance, and economics is also helpful.

What advice would you have for high school students who are interested in a profession that is similar to yours? Is there anything specific that you suggest that these high school students should do?

I would talk to people who are in the industry and have the job to learn about what they like or dislike about consulting. I would recommend getting into habits that are helpful in learning about the area, such as reading the *New York Times* business section, the *Wall Street Journal*, the *Economist*, or reading business books.

What are some aspects of your profession that the average high school student would not know but should know? What are some aspects that surprise you about your profession?

Being a good consultant requires a strong balance of many skills, such as being able to sell work to clients, but also being able to deliver projects; bringing strong financial, statistical, mathematical analysis to the table while also bringing knowledge of strategy, marketing, psychology, and operations; and being a good speaker but also being an effective listener.

If you were to hire the ideal job candidate for your profession, what kind of person would you be hiring? What qualities would this person have?

I hire people who demonstrate a problem-solving mentality; communicate effectively (written and oral); know how to lead and to follow; are confident but not cocky; and are not afraid of rolling up their sleeves to do hard work. Being able to have fun under pressure is another big plus.

Please list your favorite aspects of your profession.

Problem-solving. Diversity of challenge. Working in teams.

Please list your least-favorite aspects of your profession.

Extensive travel (potentially—I used to take 120–150 flights per year). High pressure (clients pay a lot, firms pay you a lot, and with that comes great expectations). Long hours—60-, 70-, or 80-hour weeks are closer to the norm than the exception.

STEVE TRAN

MIDDLEWARE CONSULTANT

RED HAT

Prior Roles: *Software Developer, Configuration Manager, Technical Lead.*

Education: *BS Computer Science, James Madison University; MS Computer Science, American University.*

How did you narrow down your interest(s) to your specific profession?

Consulting is a generic term that can mean anything, so, to me, I get to decide my own career path.

I picked consulting at Red Hat because I can focus on stuff I find exciting.

When did you first realize that you were interested in your profession? If this occurred during high school, how did you pursue this interest as a high school student?

I remember taking a keyboarding course in seventh grade. It was an unpopular elective at the time because people were still handwriting reports and papers. Then the TI-83 Graphing Calculator was required for a math class. Students were using them to play games, which was awesomely fascinating. My high school had an AP computer science course, so I signed up and that's how I became addicted to computers.

How did you break into the industry associated with your profession? What advice would you have for a high school student who is interested in breaking into the same industry?

I think technology is an industry where you don't need "formal" training per se. Anybody with access to the internet can take free online courses, or enroll in boot camps to quickly ramp up on subjects they are interested in.

What advice would you have for high school students who are interested in a profession that is similar to yours? Is there anything specific that you suggest that these high school students should do?

Become obsessed in technology. This industry is always evolving, so the landscape rapidly changes. Students should also program (write code) every day so that they are constantly challenged to think of new and better ways of doing something.

What are some aspects of your profession that the average high school student would not know but should know? What are some aspects that surprise you about your profession?

Even though this industry pays pretty well, this is not a career for someone who isn't truly passionate about technology. This field requires a lot of late nights, and it requires a scientific mind to solve problems. It's an absolute pleasure for those who love the industry, but it's a major headache for those who aren't in it for the right reasons.

If you were to hire the ideal job candidate for your profession, what kind of person would you be hiring? What qualities would this person have?

The ideal candidate is someone who loves to solve puzzles and other types of mental brain teasers, and someone who has a very scientific approach to problems. He/she/they should also be able to stay calm under pressure and not be afraid to dive deeply into a problem.

Please list your favorite three aspects of your profession.

My favorite part of the industry is being able to solve real problems every day. I think very few professions allow you this much freedom.

Most solutions usually fall into some sort of well-known pattern, but not every problem maps neatly to a single pattern. We need to mix and match different techniques to solve problems in an optimal way.

Please list your three least-favorite aspects about your profession.

My least-favorite part is also encountering real problems every day. What we're working on is sometimes brand-new, so we might be the first/only person to need to use technology this way. Figuring out how to do it correctly and being able to pass that knowledge onto others can be difficult.

5 DATA ANALYTICS

See the following interviews that relate to Data Analytics:

Darien Bates, Page 11

James Baldo, Page 62

DIRECTOR OF ONBOARD REVENUE STRATEGIC ANALYSIS

HOLLAND AMERICA GROUP

Prior Roles: *Senior Manager; Onboard Revenue, Strategic Analysis, and Communications Manager; Onboard Communications; Associate, GE Wind Energy.*

Education: *Master in Business Administration, Kellogg School of Management—Northwestern University; Master of Science, Civil Engineering, Stanford University; Bachelor of Science, Mechanical Engineering, MIT.*

"All models are wrong, but some are useful."

How did you narrow down your interest(s) to your specific profession?

Largely through experimentation. I tried two different fields of engineering before I decided to broaden my scope and attend business school.

When did you first realize that you were interested in your profession? If this occurred during high school, how did you pursue this interest as a high school student?

For me, it really didn't come to me until after several degrees and years in the work force.

How did you break into the industry associated with your profession? What advice would you have for a high school student who is interested in breaking into the same industry?

When you're given the opportunity to take aptitude surveys that are designed to help you understand what professions may be good for you, take them seriously.

What advice would you have for high school students who are interested in a profession that is similar to yours? Is there anything specific that you suggest that these high school students should do?

Study math and especially statistics. Once you have a good foundation in the basics, you can do a lot with it.

What are some aspects of your profession that the average high school student would not know but should know? What are some aspects that surprise you about your profession?

Ultimately, your job is to serve a business and those managing it. Often, they won't have the same level of quantitative skill as you, but they know how to earn the revenue. Humility is a virtue.

If you were to hire the ideal job candidate for your profession, what kind of person would you be hiring? What qualities would this person have?

Someone who is strong with the quantitative skill and some knowledge of IT systems but has a business mindset first and foremost.

Please list your favorite three aspects of your profession.

Collaborating with people, using math to understand human behavior, and enriching people's lives through travel.

Please list your three least-favorite aspects about your profession.

Not being able to move as fast as I would like; dealing with office politics (not unique to my profession for sure), being constrained by other departments.

How has your industry changed since the pandemic?

Clearly COVID-19 has profoundly affected all segments of the travel industry. The cruise industry, of which Holland America Group is a part, may be one of the last to recover given that so much of the early media about the pandemic was associated with cruise ships. Yet for high school students who are interested in a career in the travel industry, I believe it will be there for them when they are ready, and stronger than ever. The fundamental human desire to explore, to meet new people, and to experience new cultures is still within us. Even COVID-19 cannot squelch our curiosity in the world around us.

ELISABETH LY

SENIOR BUSINESS INTELLIGENCE REPORTING ANALYST AND DEVELOPER

Education: BS in Business Information Technology from Virginia Polytechnic Institute and State University.

"Work in progress. ;)"

How did you narrow down your interest(s) to your specific profession?

It was a natural progression that ultimately combined the enjoyable aspects of what I had been exposed to throughout my career.

When did you first realize that you were interested in your profession? If this occurred during high school, how did you pursue this interest as a high school student?

In retrospect, I have always enjoyed designing and creating things that were pretty and meaningful, but I never really considered applying that to a profession. It wasn't until much later in my career that I came to this realization.

On that note, I would encourage high school students to be aware of their interests, BUT not to feel discouraged if they don't quite know what it is just yet.

How did you break into the industry associated with your profession? What advice would you have for a high school student who is interested in breaking into the same industry?

The business intelligence (BI) world is vast, and there are many avenues to explore.

I would suggest that anyone interested in breaking into the industry (or any industry for that matter) read about the different options and play with the free tools available, if applicable. There are many different BI tools to choose from and most of them offer free editions (e.g., Microsoft Power BI

Desktop) or trial editions (e.g., Tableau) to explore. I have always been a hands-on learner and feel that this is a great way to learn.

What advice would you have for high school students who are interested in a profession that is similar to yours? Is there anything specific that you suggest that these high school students should do?

My advice to them is to play with the free tools available to them to gain knowledge.

What are some aspects of your profession that the average high school student would not know but should know? What are some aspects that surprise you about your profession?

The average high school student may not know that not all professionals who end up in the BI world started down this intended path. They should know that not all paths are set in stone and that it is THEIR personal journey to take.

If you were to hire the ideal job candidate for your profession, what kind of person would you be hiring? What qualities would this person have?

My ideal candidate would be creative, kind, astute, curious, meticulous, analytical, and genuine.

What are your favorite and least-favorite parts about your profession?

The most enjoyable aspects of my job are to design reports that are both aesthetically pleasing and insightful, to help others better understand their current environment, to ultimately make informed decisions that affect their business.

My least-favorite aspect about the world of data is that most of the time the data is not well maintained, which means that the big picture the data is representing may not be as accurate as it COULD be.

BEN PARIS

SENIOR SYSTEMS ENGINEER

SAS INSTITUTE

Prior Roles: Management Consultant—Booz Allen Hamilton; Advanced Analytics Consultant—IBM Inc.

Education: Bachelor of Science—James Madison University; Master of Business Administration—Robert H. Smith School of Business— University of Maryland.

"Pressure is what you feel when you believe you don't know what you're doing."

How did you narrow down your interest(s) to your specific profession?

It kind of evolved with the direction my career took. In a consulting position, you have to wear many hats in terms of delivering the services the client requires, and you have to evolve. When I took my first job in 2001, I was asked to do very specific simulation modeling, but over time this morphed to becoming a team leader, and getting into data warehouse work as it became part of the IT industry. From there, I once again evolved to become analytics-focused (essentially utilizing the data from those warehouses to gain actionable insights).

When did you first realize that you were interested in your profession? If this occurred during high school, how did you pursue this interest as a high school student?

It occurred in my first semester of my junior year. I knew I was interested in math and science and computers, but I had little idea in high school where this would take me. In high school, for me (in the mid-1990s), personal computers were still relatively uncommon, and home computers mostly just allowed for basic word processing and spreadsheet capabilities. The internet was only just beginning when I was in high school, with things like chat rooms and basic AOL [America

53

Online] email. I didn't know how interested I was in computer science and technology until things really exploded in my college years. Things like Napster and AIM [AOL Instant Messenger] generated my interests, and my simulation class (8 a.m. course with an awesome professor) in my junior year helped solidify what I wanted to initially start out with for a career.

How did you break into the industry associated with your profession? What advice would you have for a high school student who is interested in breaking into the same industry?

Once I found simulation modeling, I was mission-focused on finding a job where that was a primary focus. Booz Allen allowed me to start there. If you are interested in getting into computer science or any kind of analytics field, my advice would be to learn to code and start building the basic blocks of understanding open source software, such as R or Python.

Coding is a combination of art and science, so building those basic skills in high school will certainly get you started down a path. Combined with some advanced mathematics courses, you could become a basic data scientist, which is a fledgling field that can command a six-figure starting salary.

What advice would you have for high school students who are interested in a profession that is similar to yours? Is there anything specific that you suggest that these high school students should do?

STEM, STEM, STEM—There's a reason there is a huge focus on science, technology, engineering, and mathematics, and it's because those are the positions that companies always search for.

In the digital age, getting computers to work hard for you gives you a leg up on others who do not have the same skill sets. Lots of math courses, like basic statistics, are a must by junior or senior year. As mentioned previously, getting a foundation in writing code and the idea of learning programming languages are key as well.

What are some aspects of your profession that the average high school student would not know but should know? What are some aspects that surprise you about your profession?

I currently work in the big data industry. Data is the most valuable corporate asset in the world these days and governs just about every part of your life. From the moment you wake up to the moment you fall asleep (and even overnight), you are generating data both knowingly and unknowingly.

That data governs everything from what route you take to work or school, to how much you pay at a tollbooth, to what news items appear in your social media feed, to what investments your bank has made in order to pay you some measly interest rate.

Data is everywhere, and companies like SAS help every industry (SAS is in 100 percent of the Fortune 500 companies and every federal government agency) improve decision-making utilizing advanced statistics and data. SAS programs can identify whether a credit card transaction is potentially fraudulent and get your bank to call you within a few seconds of a transaction occurring anywhere in the world.

These same mathematical models and programs can determine whether someone is on a Do-Not-Fly list or other terrorist watchlist or can validate a person's identity. SAS programs also govern how to detect whether a part on a fighter jet is going to fail based on predictive analysis or which coupon to send that is most likely going to get you to walk into a specific retail establishment.

If you were to hire the ideal job candidate for your profession, what kind of person would you be hiring? What qualities would this person have?

Someone who doesn't stop asking questions and finding new and innovative ways to answer them. I look for someone who is passionate about helping others and doesn't let a little bit of adversity stop him or cause her to quit.

I come from the school of thought that you have to begin at the bottom and work your way up, which means, in some instances, you have to put your time in; those that shine in performing even the most menial of tasks are destined for greatness because of their attitude. Entitlement pisses me off—nobody is entitled to anything—so be prepared to put in long hours initially. Be the first in and the last to leave. Overdress. This speaks volumes to your character.

Please list your favorite three aspects of your profession.

Working with data—finding nuggets and trends within millions of records. Working with some of the smartest people in data science in the world, all multiple PhDs. The ability to make people's lives easier and help them deliver results with real-world impact.

Please list your three least-favorite aspects about your profession.

Politics. Turnover—sales is a high-turnover role, and, even though I'm not in a specific sales role, I work closely with the sales team. My commute to work each day is long.

6 EDUCATION

CHHAVI ARYA

TEACHER

GREATER ESSEX COUNTY DISTRICT SCHOOL BOARD

Prior Roles: *Youth Mentor & Board of Directors, Big Brothers Big Sisters Assoc. Canada; Camp Counselor; Teacher's Assistant; Youth Leader, Autism Society.*

Current Roles: *Co-Founder, Ideapress Publishing + COO/Producer, Non-Obvious Company.*

Education: *BScN, BA, BEd, University of Windsor, Ontario, Canada.*

"Decide what you hate quickly. Give up, and move onto something else. This is an underrated skill to have in life and will help you to be more successful."

— *Rohit Bhargava*

How did you narrow down your interest(s) to your specific profession?

Trial and error.

When I was in high school, I didn't know what I wanted to do for my career, but I was starting to discover what I was good at. I loved children and I gravitated to nurturing roles. At sixteen years old,

I wasn't really sure what this meant—but looking back I realize it was my first clue about what sort of career I might thrive in. Among my classes, I enjoyed both science and humanities.

For undecided students, school counselors in Canada at that time would use a standardized survey to help narrow down the options. Apparently, the desire to nurture came out in my survey responses … because the counselor suggested that I consider going into medicine. In my heart, I knew I wasn't passionate about becoming a doctor (or going to school for an additional ten years!), but a guidance counselor and several family members suggested that becoming a nurse might be a better fit. It seemed logical. Four years later, I graduated with a Bachelor of Science in Nursing. Then my life took an unexpected turn. I had landed a good job, but

I realized that I was not waking up every morning passionate and ready to do my job. I was miserable—and stuck in the wrong career. So I made a switch and went back to school.

This time, it was Teacher's College, and on the first day, I realized I had made the right choice. I was suddenly surrounded by people who loved what I loved. And I could nurture a whole new set of people with teaching.

When did you first realize that you were interested in your profession? If this occurred during high school, how did you pursue this interest as a high school student?

Soon after I started teaching, I finally realized that I've always had a desire to be an educator. What I didn't realize was that this passion for education was actually a part of something bigger … I wanted to leave a mark on the world. In my third week as a new teacher, I discovered exactly how I was going to do it.

At that time in Canada, racism was a daily event. It was not really the blatant, spit-in-your-face kind. Instead, it was baked into all the interactions around me between students, adults, teachers, the community, and the media. Sometimes it was fleeting moments, fueled by innocent ignorance. Other times it was full-blown stereotypes people shared and believed as truths. In Teacher's College, I learned that the best way to combat racism is to educate children at an early age about diverse cultures, religions, and perspectives. That became my new mission.

I became the first teacher to organize a multicultural program in my school district. I was also asked to help create a multicultural curriculum for the province of Ontario. To promote and explain the curriculum, I spoke to various educators from kindergarten to college on ways to integrate diversity into their lesson plans.

After a decade of doing what I loved, I made another big change and left the teaching profession to get married and move to the States. After having kids of my own, I developed new passions and became an entrepreneur—starting two businesses. The experience of leaving the workforce to become a mom, and then returning on my own terms to start my own businesses, reminded me that no matter what career path you choose, you always have the option to change careers.

I am currently the co-founder of two successful businesses. One is in publishing and the other is in marketing. I continued my work to teach diversity by helping to amplify diverse voices with the authors we choose to publish. It recently came full circle as I also led and produced an ambitious summit on diversity featuring more than 200 speakers called "The Non-Obvious Beyond Diversity Summit."

Learn more: www.nonobviousdiversity.com

How did you break into the industry associated with your profession? What advice would you have for a high school student who is interested in breaking into the same industry?

Listen and learn from others in the same profession. You never know who you will meet along the way.

Before I started teaching, I volunteered at an inner-city school with a kindergarten teacher. When I graduated and started looking for a job, I learned that she happened to be married to a member of the school board—and that was the connection that eventually helped me land my first teaching job.

Never stop learning.

Talk to family, friends, teachers, counselors and ask them about their experiences. Ask to shadow them at work. Build your network through social platforms such as LinkedIn. Don't be afraid to connect with those that you truly admire. You may be amazed at how many seemingly unreachable people will be happy to help out a curious and ambitious high school or college student hungry to learn.

Read.

Read to learn. Read to inspire. Read for fun. Read about topics that you don't understand and read about topics that you aren't the targeted audience for.

What advice would you have for high school students who are interested in a profession that is similar to yours? Is there anything specific that you suggest that these high school students should do?

Find your fire, what drives you, what excites you, and choose activities that fuel that fire, passion, and drive. But remember that passion may change as you grow.

Most people don't have the same career they had ten years ago. People change, so don't feel locked into any college or career right now. Don't be afraid to leave the career path you're on behind and go in a different direction.

JAMES BALDO

ASSOCIATE PROFESSOR AND DIRECTOR OF THE MS DATA ANALYTICS PROGRAM

GEORGE MASON UNIVERSITY

Prior Roles: Data Architect, Enterprise Architect, Director of Software Development, Software Engineer.

Education: BS Chemistry, MS Chemistry, MS Computer Engineering, PhD Software Engineering.

How did you narrow down your interest(s) to your specific profession?

During my undergraduate years, I was involved with interfacing chemical instrumentation to minicomputers. I acquired a large amount of knowledge and experience with both hardware (interfacing the instrument to the computer) and software (analytical calculations on the acquired data). I continued to work in this area during my chemistry MS as the focus of my master's thesis. My first job was interfacing communications test harnesses to telecommunications switches, which motivated me to obtain an engineering degree. I was able to test out of a number of graduate engineering entry-level courses and obtain my master's in computer engineering. During this time, my interests became more focused on software engineering methods and associated analysis and theory. I decided to pursue my PhD in software engineering in the area of software architectures.

When did you first realize that you were interested in your profession? If this occurred during high school, how did you pursue this interest as a high school student?

Most likely during my undergraduate years. My mentor realized that my interests in both hardware and software were divergent, and he strongly recommended I select one. This was my turning point. Still, my interests in software at this time were extremely broad. One extreme was programming development and another extreme was a computational science.

How did you break into the industry associated with your profession? What advice would you have for a high school student who is interested in breaking into the same industry?

I needed a job, and my skills were in high demand. I was also fortunate to find many positions that were very interesting and provided opportunities to learn and enhance my knowledge and experience.

What advice would you have for high school students who are interested in a profession that is similar to yours? Is there anything specific that you suggest that these high school students should do?

Always follow your interests and focus not only on the big picture, but also make sure to study and understand the details, no matter how small.

What are some aspects of your profession that the average high school student would not know but should know? What are some aspects that surprise you about your profession?

My area of interest requires a strong background in statistics/probability, computer science/software engineering, and calculus. I am constantly reviewing these areas.

Also, it is important to maintain high ethical standards and develop a feeling of confidence for your work.

Having a solid foundation in the fundamentals of your chosen area will give you this confidence.

If you were to hire the ideal job candidate for your profession, what kind of person would you be hiring? What qualities would this person have?

Here is my list:

- Motivation
- Ethics
- Strong educational background
- Practical approach to problem-solving
- Experience (yes, younger candidates may be shallow in this area; however, discussing projects and interests are a good indicator)
- Ability to work in a team environment

Please provide a quote or mantra that you feel accurately reflects both you and your profession. It can be a quote generated by you or a quote from someone else.

Good question. This is my best response: be ethical, have thoroughness with respect to problem-solving, learn from your mistakes, and consider innovation.

Please list your favorite three aspects of your profession.

1. Problem-solving
2. Innovation
3. Learning

Please list your three least-favorite aspects about your profession.

1. Difficulties with managing teams
2. Being given problems that employers feel are easy
3. Reporting failure (which is part of the job)

RYAN GROVE

SUBJECT EXPERT TEACHER (MATH AND PHYSICS)

BASIS INDEPENDENT MCLEAN

Education: BS, Physics, Indiana University of Pennsylvania; BS, Applied Mathematics, Indiana University of Pennsylvania; MS, Applied Mathematics, Indiana University of Pennsylvania; PhD, Mathematical Sciences, Clemson University.

"Life is much too important a thing ever to talk seriously about it."

— Oscar Wilde

How did you narrow down your interest(s) to your specific profession?

I wanted to make sure that every morning that I woke up, I was excited to go to work doing a job that I actually enjoyed.

When did you first realize that you were interested in your profession? If this occurred during high school, how did you pursue this interest as a high school student?

I didn't realize I liked teaching until graduate school, and not until after trying various other job areas first.

How did you break into the industry associated with your profession? What advice would you have for a high school student who is interested in breaking into the same industry?

Networking was the biggest factor. Make sure you get out there and people know about you, as well as about the good work you are doing.

Go to conferences, present your work, and make many friends in the community that you are interested in.

What advice would you have for high school students who are interested in a profession that is similar to yours? Is there anything specific that you suggest that these high school students should do?

Do it! Teaching is the best. It requires you to accept that you won't be super rich (which I realize is hard to do for many kids, especially in very competitive areas such as Northern Virginia), but it's a genuinely rewarding job that you can feel great about day after day. You just have to weigh everything about a career before you make a decision about how you would like to spend the rest of your life.

Don't be afraid to be wrong; I was wrong about what I wanted to do many times before I found something I loved doing.

What are some aspects of your profession that the average high school student would not know but should know? What are some aspects that surprise you about your profession?

It's a lot of work. It's completely worth it, though.

If you were to hire the ideal job candidate for your profession, what kind of person would you be hiring? What qualities would this person have?

Someone who shows passion and perseverance.

Please list your favorite three aspects of your profession.

Impact. Fun. Teaching.

Please list your three least-favorite aspects about your profession.

Grading cubed.

How has your industry changed since the pandemic?

Seeing students in the classroom is one of my favorite parts of being a teacher, so it kind of sucks. That being said, it's important to be able to adapt to all kinds of situations, especially in these times. Now, more than ever, trying new things, learning from your mistakes, and trying to help the students to the best of your abilities are crucial to the success of your students.

Additional Comments:

Find something that you will enjoy pouring your heart into.

KATE IRVING

COLLEGE COUNSELOR

BASIS INDEPENDENT MCLEAN

Prior Roles: *Director of After School Programming at Boys and Girls Club of America; English Teacher in NYC Department of Education; Adjunct Professor and Activities Coordinator at Kogod School of Business, American University.*

Education: *Saint Mary's College of California; BA in English Teachers College, Columbia University; MA in Teaching, Hunter College; MS in Education in School Counseling.*

"Be you. The more genuine we are with ourselves and others, the more clear our education, personal, and career paths will be."

How did you narrow down your interest(s) to your specific profession?

I narrowed my interests through experience. When I was in college, I followed my passion for English and became a teacher. While teaching, I followed my passion for helping students through high school and into college and became a college counselor.

When did you first realize that you were interested in your profession? If this occurred during high school, how did you pursue this interest as a high school student?

My passion for teaching and counseling did not begin in high school. As a high school student, I knew I wanted to go to a liberal arts college so I could explore all areas of study. I had no idea what I wanted to be. Through the diversity of my college courses and the collaborative learning experiences I encountered, I found my specific interest in writing essays, examining literature, and teaching others.

How did you break into the industry associated with your profession? What advice would you have for a high school student who is interested in breaking into the same industry?

While in New York City, I took the required teaching courses and tests to become certified to teach high school. I interviewed at many schools in the NYC area and began my career at a small, college readiness-focused school in the Bronx. When I wanted to transition into counseling, I attended a masters program for school counseling, took all of the required courses and tests, and interviewed at several programs throughout the city until I found my match. Do the work, check the requirements, and then find a school that fits into your educational and personal beliefs.

What advice would you have for high school students who are interested in a profession that is similar to yours? Is there anything specific that you suggest that these high school students should do?

My advice is to find your passion and then to share it with as many professors, family, friends, and professionals as you can.

The more people you can discuss your career aspirations with, the more chances they will be able to guide you on your way. Network with the idea of meeting new people. Do not network with the specific intention of getting a job or internship. This focus will make you more genuine and open to the variety of options life has to offer.

What are some aspects of your profession that the average high school student would not know but should know? What are some aspects that surprise you about your profession?

What surprised me the most from teaching and counseling is the amount of work that I take home. My days are filled interacting with and teaching students, and it is only when I am home that I can create my plan for the day, week, or month.

If you were to hire the ideal job candidate for your profession, what kind of person would you be hiring? What qualities would this person have?

The person would have to be genuine and want to help others. Someone who is student-focused and not just working to check the boxes is ready for this kind of work. Time management and the ability to manage multiple tasks at once is also a necessary skill. The person would also have to like teenagers.

Please list your favorite three aspects of your profession.

Human interaction. Tangible results. Involvement in the pursuit of students' dreams.

Please list your three least-favorite aspects about your profession.

Pressure for results. Time spent working outside of work hours. When students are denied to a college.

MONICA ISQUITH

SUBJECT EXPERT TEACHER (SCIENCE)

BASIS INDEPENDENT MCLEAN

Prior Roles: *Head of the Science Department in a private school.*

Education: *I graduated with a doctorate in dental medicine from The Dental School in Colombia, South America.*

"Seize the day."

How did you narrow down your interest(s) to your specific profession?

I always have loved working with kids, and I like the health and science fields.

When did you first realize that you were interested in your profession? If this occurred during high school, how did you pursue this interest as a high school student?

In high school, I realized that I wanted to be in the health field, and when I was in dental school, I loved tutoring and helping other students in class by explaining concepts.

How did you break into the industry associated with your profession? What advice would you have for a high school student who is interested in breaking into the same industry?

I would advise my students to join clubs and volunteer in different fields, so, that way, the student can try to find his/her/their true interest.

What advice would you have for high school students who are interested in a profession that is similar to yours? Is there anything specific that you suggest that these high school students should do?

I would tell them to research each field of interest so that they have the information needed to choose the right area of study.

Please list your favorite three aspects of your profession.

Working with people, changing lives, and inspiring others.

Please list your three least-favorite aspects about your profession.

Bureaucracy.

Additional Comments:

Follow your passions!

SCOTT McINTOSH

TENNIS PROGRAM MANAGER AND TENNIS PROFESSIONAL

4 STAR TENNIS ACADEMY OF VIRGINIA

Prior Roles: Camp Director, Camp Counselor, Director Assistant, Bus Driver, and Tennis Director.

Education: Bachelor's Degree in Economics and Accounting from Ohio University.

"You have to believe in the long-term plan you have, but you need the short-term goals to motivate and inspire you."

— Roger Federer

How did you narrow down your interest(s) to your specific profession?

When I graduated from school, I decided to move back home from Ohio. The first thing I decided after that was to check out the YMCA with Coach Mel Labat. I started out part time in Bethesda and when the winter came, Mel decided to bring me in to the Arlington YMCA, and that is when my career really started.

When did you first realize that you were interested in your profession? If this occurred during high school, how did you pursue this interest as a high school student?

I started out with my interest when I was in seventh grade and Coach Mel gave me a position to teach. I love teaching kids, and I really had a feel for coaching. I loved dealing with parents and kids alike and helping them grow in the sport.

How did you break into the industry associated with your profession? What advice would you have for a high school student who is interested in breaking into the same industry?

I broke in when Mel gave me that opportunity to work indoors as his assistant and have grown each year since then.

What advice would you have for high school students who are interested in a profession that is similar to yours? Is there anything specific that you suggest that these high school students should do?

I would say to learn as much about the sport of tennis as possible and to get certified. Take classes, volunteer, and shadow pros.

What are some aspects of your profession that the average high school student would not know but should know? What are some aspects that surprise you about your profession?

It's not as easy as it may seem to get into the profession. Although you do not need a degree, the amount of space at most tennis clubs is very limited. A lot of tennis is weather-permitting, so if you are teaching outside, you can only teach for three seasons, and if it rains, you are out for the day.

If you were to hire the ideal job candidate for your profession, what kind of person would you be hiring? What qualities would this person have?

Trustworthy, comes on time, and shows up every day. Very knowledgeable about the sport, and has a great attitude.

Please list your favorite three aspects of your profession.

1. Seeing clients learn and seeing that light turn on in their head and on the court.
2. Camaraderie with the other coaches with a great work environment.
3. Just being able to help a child who may not have help at home and making them smile.

Please list your three least-favorite aspects about your profession.

1. Cleaning up tennis balls.
2. Difficult students, adults, and children alike.
3. Balancing administrative work and court time.

RONALD SEYB

ASSOCIATE DEAN OF THE FACULTY FOR STUDENT ACADEMIC AFFAIRS AND ASSOCIATE PROFESSOR OF POLITICAL SCIENCE

SKIDMORE COLLEGE

Education: University of California at Irvine,
BA in Political Science and Psychology; Yale University, MA, MPhil, and PhD.

How did you narrow down your interest(s) to your specific profession?

I did not entertain a number of different career options. I drifted into this career because my undergraduate advisor, for reasons that remain puzzling to me, thought that I could pursue a career as an academic. I confess that, even at the conclusion of my senior year in college, I still did not have even spectral notions about how I wanted to earn a living. If you had approached me at that time and asked me about my career aspirations, I likely would have given you the same response that I gave to people who asked me when I was five years old what I wanted to be when I grew up: "a cowboy or an astronaut."

When did you first realize that you were interested in your profession? If this occurred during high school, how did you pursue this interest as a high school student?

I did not really become interested in ideas until the tail end of my freshman year in college. It was then that it occurred to me that forming arguments was as much a creative process as "dabbling in oil paints and colors so rare." I spent most of my adolescence either playing sports or finding other ways to slip the surly bonds of books. It was hence a revelation to me that books could be as exciting and transformative as an athletic endeavor.

72

How did you break into the industry associated with your profession? What advice would you have for a high school student who is interested in breaking into the same industry?

I did not understand when I applied to graduate school just how few jobs there are in academia. I thus feel exceptionally fortunate to have been gifted with an academic position at such a tender age (an age when I clearly did not have even the thinnest of notions about what was expected of me and was blithely unaware of how woefully ill-equipped I was to meet those expectations).

High school students who may be contemplating becoming a college professor should hence be mindful of how competitive the academic job market is (though, of course, the fierceness of the competition differs across disciplines and even among subdisciplines within a discipline). For example, in political science, we usually receive north of 150 applications for any open position.

What advice would you have for high school students who are interested in a profession that is similar to yours? Is there anything specific that you suggest that these high school students should do?

If a high school student wishes to become a teacher, whether that is a college professor or an elementary school instructor, the most important thing to do is develop curiosity. Apropos skills, poor writing is the most conspicuous deficit sported by people entering the workforce. Learning how to write clearly, grammatically, and economically will serve a student in any chosen profession.

What are some aspects of your profession that the average high school student would not know but should know? What are some aspects that surprise you about your profession?

Students see only a small portion of a faculty member's professional life. The publishing demands are quite real, relentless, and even ornery (i.e., they do not allow one to rest even after a taxing day in the classroom). College faculty, however, are also expected to serve on committees and task forces that can vacuum up a considerable amount of their time (and good vibrations). People entering this profession hence need to learn quickly how to balance sometimes competing imperatives in a way that preserves their mental hygiene without angering or disappointing their colleagues and constituents.

If you were to hire the ideal job candidate for your profession, what kind of person would you be hiring? What qualities would this person have?

The ideal job candidate is one who can formulate questions and arguments. I find that some of my younger colleagues are reluctant to take intellectual or professional risks. Many of them complete what my wife calls "homework assignments" that are doled out by their dissertation advisors or some other mentor. This is the smoothest path to publication. It is also, however, the road to the perdition of pedestrian work.

What are your favorite and least-favorite parts about your profession?

The favorite part of my job is watching students develop both intellectually and emotionally during their time at Skidmore and after they leave the sacred sod here. The least-favorite part of my job is the large number of meetings that are designed, at least to my mind, to find reasons to support or justify decisions that have already been made. This Jesuit approach to college governance is, as the journalist David Halberstam once said about his time covering the Congo War, a time when he endured scorching heat, regular malarial invasions, and frequent hostile fire, "bad for morale."

How has your industry changed since the pandemic?

The COVID-19 pandemic may be fomenting the paradigm shift that higher education has been flirting with for some time. When Thomas Kuhn introduced the concept of paradigm change in *The Structure of Scientific Revolutions* back in 1962, he maintained that such a tectonic shift in thinking is invariably preceded by a period of "normal science," during which practitioners try to fill cracks in the foundation of the old paradigm rather than risk the career-disabling consequences of adopting a completely new set of questions, concepts, and theories ("Science advances one funeral at a time.").

Higher education has been in a period of normal science for some time, patching the cracks in its foundation with ideas such as "skills-based instruction," "globalized education," and "experiential and integrative learning." The failed experiment in remote education, however, seems to be generating the reckoning that the resistance to paradigm change usually thwarts. Liberal arts college administrators now must try to cultivate a faculty that can deliver high-quality instruction regardless of the modality.

My colleagues and I have been spending the past months trying to discern how residential colleges will continue to thrive in an environment in which residential life appears to be untenable for the foreseeable future. How can we give students a liberal arts education when the classroom is virtual and the interactions among students are mediated? Are there standards of instruction to which all faculty must adhere in order to ensure that every student is receiving an educational experience that is commensurate with their families' financial investment and their desire to learn? Will both faculties and student bodies need to shrink in order to provide this education? If they do, then what is the new financial model for small liberal arts colleges? Needless to say, the answers to all of these questions are unclear. Kuhn argued, however, that such opacity can be the precursor to a major shift of thinking. On the other hand, normal science can continue well past the moment when its diminishing returns place the entire enterprise in jeopardy.

Higher education now has an opportunity to slip the fetters of normal science. Whether it will do so will depend a great deal on college administrators' appetite for risk and college faculties' willingness to accept that the stakes are existential.

KARL ULRICH

PROFESSOR

UNIVERSITY OF PENNSYLVANIA

Education: SB MIT Mechanical Engineering, SM MIT Mechanical Engineering, ScD MIT Mechanical Engineering.

"Always choose the path that will teach you the most."

How did you narrow down your interest(s) to your specific profession?

At each career-decision point, I chose the path that involved more learning (usually more school) until I had to choose a job in industry or a job in academics—I chose academics because it was the most flexible, most interesting option. I was always interested in innovation, design, and business. So, I chose to teach in that area.

When did you first realize that you were interested in your profession? If this occurred during high school, how did you pursue this interest as a high school student?

I suspected I would be interested in an academic career sometime during my undergraduate studies. My parents were professors so I understood the advantages of the job.

How did you break into the industry associated with your profession? What advice would you have for a high school student who is interested in breaking into the same industry?

If you want to be a professor, you need to get very good at learning on your own. Writing and speaking skills are also very important. But, basically be interested in learning and do really well in school.

What are some aspects of your profession that the average high school student would not know but should know? What are some aspects that surprise you about your profession?

Professors at top institutions work very long hours (basically all the time), but this work is something they really enjoy, so it's not really work.

If you were to hire the ideal job candidate for your profession, what kind of person would you be hiring? What qualities would this person have?

Independent, can get things done on his/her/their own initiative. Curious about the world.

Please list your favorite three aspects of your profession.

1. Complete autonomy to do what I want.
2. Teaching young people.
3. Surrounded by smart people.

Please list your three least-favorite aspects about your profession.

Grading is the only thing I don't like.

Additional Comments:

Professors have very different experiences based on (a) status of institution, and (b) field. A biology professor at East Hopscotch State University will have a very different life than a business professor at Stanford.

VERN WILLIAMS

SUBJECT EXPERT TEACHER (MATH)

BASIS INDEPENDENT MCLEAN

Prior Roles: *Math Teacher in Fairfax County Public Schools.*

Education: *BS Math Education, University of Maryland.*

"Math is not only about things that are useful but about things that are cool."

— *Kevin Casto (former teaching assistant of Vern Williams)*

How did you narrow down your interest(s) to your specific profession?

I went through every occupation, from FBI agent to oceanographer. None impressed me more than teaching because I had outstanding junior high school teachers.

When did you first realize that you were interested in your profession? If this occurred during high school, how did you pursue this interest as a high school student?

I realized that I wanted to become a teacher while attending junior high school (grades 7–9). I made certain that I took high school courses appropriate for college-bound students, such as Modern European History, instead of Typing.

How did you break into the industry associated with your profession? What advice would you have for a high school student who is interested in breaking into the same industry?

The teaching profession is easy to break into since, in many venues, there are teacher shortages. However, math/science, foreign language, and special education teachers are in higher demand than some other specialties, such as English and elementary education. You, of course, can major in education, which leads to student teaching, and, more than likely, a teaching position. You can also major in a specific subject, such as math, and then take the appropriate education courses.

What advice would you have for high school students who are interested in a profession that is similar to yours? Is there anything specific that you suggest that these high school students should do?

In the case of teaching, I would suggest becoming a tutor as part of a community service project or pursuing a position in an established tutoring service. Some tutoring services happily hire high school students. One can also apply as a teaching assistant (either volunteer or paid) to summer academic camps. Such camps range from those such as the Johns Hopkins Center for Talented Youth (CTY) to camps for students with special needs.

What are some aspects of your profession that the average high school student would not know but should know? What are some aspects that surprise you about your profession?

They should know that teaching is very difficult and demanding work if done well. They should also know that the pay is not high compared to many other professions requiring a college degree.

The surprise will be that many schools have very little DNA in common with the school that they attend. They will also discover that many of the financial resources delegated to schools do not necessarily end up in the classroom.

If you were to hire the ideal job candidate for your profession, what kind of person would you be hiring? What qualities would this person have?

I actually run a summer math enrichment camp. I hire teaching assistants who want to share their love of learning with everyone, everywhere, all the time. They are able to explain content in a nonthreatening way, and they make their students feel that learning is cool.

One of my former teaching assistants (when he was in high school), who just received a math degree from Brown University, stated the following when one of the summer campers asked when a certain concept would be useful in real life. His answer was priceless. "Math is not only about things that are useful but about things that are cool." The following year I included his quote on the back of the camp T-shirt.

It also helps to have a warm, caring personality. I still remember my fifth-grade teacher whose main goal in life was to be bitter toward kids and other living things.

Please list your favorite three aspects of your profession.

Knowing that each exciting day will be totally different from the day before. Helping students to become fantastic young adults. Personally learning more about math (at times from my students) than I ever thought possible.

Please list your three least-favorite aspects about your profession.

Dealing with the K–12 education bureaucracy. Watching K–12 education become highly politicized over the last forty years. A decline in educational standards in the US.

How has your industry changed since the pandemic?

COVID-19 has definitely changed the face of education. The residing question is whether it will be a temporary change. Distance learning in various forms has become the norm, and there seems to be very little indication that things will return to "the old" normal anytime soon. For some students at my school, it has been a struggle keeping track of assignments and expectations without the usual in-class supervision. For a few students, improvement over the in-class experience has occurred because they are allowed to complete assignments on their own time schedule. For some independent self-motivated learners, distance learning has actually enhanced their overall learning experience.

So I view distance learning at this point as a mixed bag, but I expect major improvements as both teachers and students learn to navigate the technology and manage expectations. When COVID-19 is long gone and forgotten, some facets of distance learning will remain part of the landscape. As for me personally, I have never worked harder. I hold live sessions daily with all of my classes, and the amount of preparation is almost overwhelming. I am indeed thankful that, unlike decades ago, we have the technology that allows students to interact with both their teachers and peers. I am more than willing to perform the extra work so that students can have productive live sessions. I view those sessions as much more important than videos, websites, and other resources because connections and relationships for many students are of paramount importance. In fact, such connections and relationships highly enhance learning.

Additional Comments:

I have been teaching for over forty years, and I have never had even one regret.

7 ENGINEERING

See the following interviews that relate to Engineering:

Ben Paris, Page 53

James Baldo, Page 62

Tom Burket, Page 145

WESLEY BURGHARDT

PROFESSOR OF CHEMICAL AND BIOLOGICAL ENGINEERING

NORTHWESTERN UNIVERSITY

Prior Roles: I worked as a research and teaching assistant during my graduate studies, which helped prepare me for my current role. I also had a short summer job working for a chemical company in Germany over a summer while I was an undergraduate student.

Education: BS, Chemical Engineering, 1985, University of Illinois, Urbana, IL; MS, Chemical Engineering, 1986, University of Illinois, Urbana, IL; PhD, Chemical Engineering, 1991, Stanford University, Stanford, CA.

How did you narrow down your interest(s) to your specific profession?

I chose chemical engineering as my college major based on my affinity for math and science. As I got deeper into my studies, I was drawn more towards the fundamental aspects of the field and opportunities for research. This led me, progressively, towards decisions to pursue graduate study, and ultimately to pursue an academic career as a university professor.

When did you first realize that you were interested in your profession? If this occurred during high school, how did you pursue this interest as a high school student?

The particular choice of chemical engineering was a bit random. My father (an architect) did some design work for a company that made chemical process equipment, and the person who was his primary contact at that company happened to be a chemical engineer. One day he mentioned to me that "XXX is a chemical engineer, and he seems pretty sharp; maybe you should think about studying that." This, more or less, is what nudged me in this particular direction, although it was consistent with the fact that I liked chemistry. I didn't really pursue this any further in high school, except to take a full load of AP math/science courses.

How did you break into the industry associated with your profession? What advice would you have for a high school student who is interested in breaking into the same industry?

As previously indicated, once I was a student in college, my progression towards my ultimate career as a professor evolved naturally, as a result of opportunities I was given. Certainly participation in undergraduate research had a big impact on my decision to pursue further research as a PhD student. And, opportunities to get involved in teaching and mentoring other students during my graduate career influenced my decision to pursue teaching. I guess one thing important to understand is that becoming a college professor in engineering requires that one pursue education through the PhD level. This is a lot to think about as a high school student, but you don't have to commit to this right from the start. I think once you're in a college environment, you will come to better understand the role of university faculty, and whether this line of work aligns with your interests and goals.

What advice would you have for high school students who are interested in a profession that is similar to yours? Is there anything specific that you suggest that these high school students should do?

As an engineer, the most important advice is pretty self-evident, namely that you should pursue a healthy diet of math and science courses in high school.

Many schools offer engineering-related courses, or computer programming. If you have the chance to do either, this will help give you a better sense for whether or not engineering feels right for you. Somewhat less obviously, I would encourage students interested in engineering to take some kind of shop class to begin learning practical skills of how to build things.

As an educator, look for opportunities to work with your classmates, trying to help them understand things. Or, see if there are tutoring opportunities in your school or community.

You might find, like me, that helping someone understand difficult topics and progress in their mastery of a subject can be extremely rewarding.

What are some aspects of your profession that the average high school student would not know but should know? What are some aspects that surprise you about your profession?

I guess the most important thing is to understand that, in most engineering schools, faculty have diverse responsibilities that extend well beyond classroom teaching.

In fact, relative to high school teachers, we spend relatively little time teaching. The major activity that occupies our time, in addition to teaching, is research and scholarship. It is part of our core job description to pursue research projects to advance our understanding of whatever field we pursue (chemical engineering, in my case). This involves background work of reading research papers published by others; deciding what new problem is worth pursuing; writing proposals to government agencies, foundations, or companies to get the funding necessary to pursue the research; supervising graduate students who are typically the main people who actually do the work; and writing papers and attending professional conferences to share the results of the work with the broader community.

Something that surprised me when I was starting out in my job is the fact that, while I was trained primarily as a researcher during my

PhD studies, the things that one actually does as a faculty member (teaching, supervising students, raising funds, etc.) are quite a bit different.

If you were to hire the ideal job candidate for your profession, what kind of person would you be hiring? What qualities would this person have?

When we recruit faculty, we seek candidates who are working in exciting fields of research, who have a proven record of success in their past work, and who have intriguing ideas for their future research directions. They must show a high level of technical mastery of their field and, critically, must have the ability to communicate what they do and what they have learned effectively in both written and oral formats. (Effective communication is essential for the teaching requirements of academic positions.) Finally, it is important that candidates convince us that they are enthusiastic and will be willing to do their share of service to help keep the university running smoothly.

Please provide a quote or mantra that you feel accurately reflects both you and your profession. It can be a quote generated by you or a quote from someone else.

I forget, unfortunately, the origin of this quip, but I've always liked it:

"Universities are full of knowledge. Students come in knowing a little, and they leave knowing less. Thus, the knowledge accumulates."

I don't actually subscribe to this, of course, but I like how it (probably unwittingly) draws upon one of the foundational concepts from chemical engineering, a general conservation law:

Accumulation = input - output + generation - consumption.

Please list your favorite three aspects of your profession.

1. Teaching and working with students.
2. The freedom to define and pursue my personal research interests (so long as I can raise the necessary funds).
3. Academic life, in general, is very pleasant, being surrounded by smart and creative people, developing relationships with fellow researchers from around the country and around the world, etc.

Please list your three least-favorite aspects about your profession.

1. It appears my days get highly congested with meetings; this is exacerbated by the fact that I also hold an administrative position at my university.
2. Research funding is increasingly difficult to come by.
3. One of my specific responsibilities is investigating academic integrity violations (i.e., cheating). This isn't much fun.

ATISH GHOSH

SENIOR VICE PRESIDENT OF GLOBAL RESEARCH AND DEVELOPMENT

ELLUCIAN

Prior Roles: Group Vice President, Product Development; Director, Product Development; Manager, Product Development; Senior Developer.

Education: BS Electrical Engineering (EE), Clemson University; MS EE, Clemson University; PhD EE, Clemson University.

"There is a science and art to engineering."

How did you narrow down your interest(s) to your specific profession?

I was always very interested in physics and math through high school. I found them easy to learn and do well in, in school. I chose electrical engineering as my undergraduate degree as that was the closest degree that combined my interest in physics and math, and I believe I got advice to pick engineering as a more "practical" option. The first course I ever took about computers in college is what got me hooked onto computing, and I was always very interested in coding after that. Even though I went on to graduate school and got a PhD

and enjoyed the research aspect of graduate school, I always knew that I wanted to write code when I started work. I loved creating software.

When did you first realize that you were interested in your profession? If this occurred during high school, how did you pursue this interest as a high school student?

I had never used a computer until very late in high school and actually had a really tough time in my first computer class ever. I took it among kids who had been using a computer for some time, whereas I had absolutely zero exposure to it and did not know the basics. I ended up dropping out of this class as everyone else was clearly far ahead of me, and I was struggling (it was an optional high school class). This was in the UK. My next computer class was in college, where I was taught Fortran, and that's when I really learned computer programming, really enjoyed it, and "aced" the class. This was the first time I really got interested in computing.

How did you break into the industry associated with your profession? What advice would you have for a high school student who is interested in breaking into the same industry?

My first job was in a company that created software for the electric power industry. It combined my expertise in electrical engineering and the electric power industry, as well as my background and interest in computer science/software. It was a natural fit for me given my background and work in graduate school. Computing and software is ubiquitous now with absolutely no shortage of demand for anyone who wants to be a software developer and write software. If you are interested in the software industry, I would suggest trying to find some part-time/internship opportunities in the industry to better understand the work.

What advice would you have for high school students who are interested in a profession that is similar to yours? Is there anything specific that you suggest that these high school students should do?

For high school students who are interested in computers and/or anything IT-related, I would say that it's a great option. Practically speaking, I expect that opportunities and jobs will continue to grow in IT-related fields. My biggest advice would be to make sure it is something that you really enjoy doing. If possible, I would suggest finding a family member, family friend, or neighbor in the field and talk to them about their job in more detail.

What are some aspects of your profession that the average high school student would not know but should know? What are some aspects that surprise you about your profession?

What you do when you first start work and where you end up later in your work life can be very different.

My work is very different today than what it was over twenty years ago when I first started. I started my career writing software as that is what I loved back then. As my career evolved, I got more involved in leading and managing teams and found that I could be good at that while still enjoying coding.

I hit a point in my career where I had to finally decide to commit to management and leadership, which took my career in a different direction to where it is today. The skills I need to succeed in management and leadership are totally different than the skills I relied on when I first started work.

In almost all industries, you can either be an individual contributor with a specific skill (football player, developer, creative artist, accountant, pilot, etc.) or you can get involved in leadership, management, and entrepreneurial aspects of that industry/expertise (coach, manager/executive, producer, executive/business owner, colonel).

I had no idea about this when I was in high school or college. Learning to listen, communicate (both verbal and written), working as a team, and taking initiative are all great skills/habits that apply to all professions.

Being self-aware is probably ultimately one of the most important aspects as you think about any profession—what are you interested in, what do you want out of life?

If you were to hire the ideal job candidate for your profession, what kind of person would you be hiring? What qualities would this person have?

The most common qualities I look for in candidates, regardless of the role/level and beyond their specific experience/expertise requirements, are being high energy, having innate curiosity, and being articulate and flexible.

CHRIS GREAMO

PRESIDENT AND CHIEF EXECUTIVE OFFICER

TWO SIX LABS

Prior Roles: *Executive Vice President, Invincea Labs; Chief Engineer and Director, Network Defense Products, BAE Systems; Principal Research Engineer, Alphatech; Senior Development Manager, Manugistics; Research Engineer, Thomson Corporation; Member of Technical Staff, TASC.*

Education: *Bachelor of Science in Electrical Engineering, Carnegie Mellon University; Master of Science in Electrical Engineering, Massachusetts Institute of Technology.*

"Great things in business are never done by one person. They're done by a team of people."

— Steve Jobs

How did you narrow down your interest(s) to your specific profession?

I had a deep interest in science and technology from the earliest age that I can remember. From elementary school, I always knew that I wanted to pursue a career in science or engineering. Starting in high school, I took a strong interest in electronics, including a deep interest in computer programming (particularly assembly and C). I was lucky enough to have a great physics teacher in high school, Dr. Newburg. Dr. Newburg had degrees in physics from

Harvard and MIT and had a very successful career working on research and development projects for the Department of Defense. The stories that he told about his work were inspiring, and I knew that I wanted to pursue a similar career path. Originally, I had planned to study physics in college but decided to change to electrical engineering since it was a better fit for the skills that I would need to acquire, as well as a better fit based on my interest in computer programming.

When did you first realize that you were interested in your profession? If this occurred during high school, how did you pursue this interest as a high school student?

As I described above, I always knew that I wanted a career in science and technology. I narrowed down the scope to engineering, particularly electrical engineering, in high school, thanks to the help of my high school physics teacher.

I did pursue opportunities as a high school intern. For two years (summers after eleventh and twelfth grades), I was able to get jobs writing software programs for local small businesses to help them automate their business processes. These opportunities not only helped me greatly advance my software engineering and programming skills but also introduced me to the business process and how companies operated, which helped me later on in my career.

How did you break into the industry associated with your profession? What advice would you have for a high school student who is interested in breaking into the same industry?

My break came after my freshman year of college/ undergrad. My father happened to see an ad in one of the Boston-area papers. One of the companies in the area, TASC, was holding a recruiting event for summer interns. TASC was a government contracting firm that did advanced research and development for the Department of Defense, so I decided to attend the event and apply.

I was accepted into the program and had an incredible blast working for the company that summer. As a result, I wound up returning every summer (and some winter breaks) throughout my college career. This allowed me to build a professional network of colleagues that I met and worked with throughout my time as an intern.

With the exception of one position in my career, all of the positions/jobs that I've had throughout my career have been through referrals from colleagues, many of whom tie directly back to people that I met and worked with during those years as an intern. A strong professional network is key, and this was true long before the creation of the internet and social networking platforms, like LinkedIn. I didn't know it at the time, but that professional network would directly or indirectly influence nearly every other career opportunity that I've had, including my first full-time job and my current position at Two Six Labs.

What advice would you have for high school students who are interested in a profession that is similar to yours? Is there anything specific that you suggest that these high school students should do?

Find opportunities to do internships. At Two Six Labs, for example, we regularly hire high school interns. Folks can apply at www.twosixlabs.com/ careers or send an email to info@twosixlabs.com. There are many other technology companies in the area that have similar programs. Search them out.

Do side projects on your own time. When we interview a high school candidate for an internship, describing a cool side project that you've done on your own time is the best way to impress the hiring manager. Not only does it show that you have a passion for the field, but it is the best way for someone with no other work experience to demonstrate that he/she/they has some skills.

Get your name out there, and start building your own brand. With the internet, it is much easier these days for high school students to start to create a professional name for themselves. Take advantage of that. Submit code to GitHub or open source projects. Create a LinkedIn profile. Write blogs on technology areas that you find interesting and have a passion. Join competitions, like CTFs (Capture the Flag), or hackathons.

What are some aspects of your profession that the average high school student would not know but should know? What are some aspects that surprise you about your profession?

There is a misguided belief that technology professionals (particularly IT professionals, software engineers and computer scientists) don't need to have good verbal and written communication skills.

People think of the Dilbert-like character who spends his days in front of a computer screen, cranking out code. This is a fallacy.

Successful engineers and scientists (particularly those that rise to senior technical positions in companies) spend the majority of their days in meetings with colleagues, customers, partners, etc. You actually spend your "nights and weekends" cranking the code. :)

To be successful, you must have the ability to both write and speak professionally (including publicly). So, while science, math, and engineering are incredibly important, don't neglect or discount the importance of English, language, and other humanities-type classes.

If your school offers them, take classes/electives in journalism. Join the debate team. Take a part in school plays. The communication skills that you learn in these activities, you'll find, will help you greatly, even in a technology career.

If you were to hire the ideal job candidate for your profession, what kind of person would you be hiring? What qualities would this person have?

- Insatiable curiosity.

- Ability to work well with others. Experience with being part of a team.
- Good communication skills.
- Confidence.
- A sense of humor.

Please list your favorite three aspects of your profession.

1. The technology (particularly the technology R&D) profession attracts really smart and interesting people. No matter where you work in this industry, you typically get the opportunity to work with really smart and strong teams of people.

2. The ability to make significant impacts to the world and your customers.

3. The fact that technology development is a team sport.

Please list your three least-favorite aspects about your profession.

1. Particularly in the government R&D space, decisions on which technology ideas are pursued and which are not are too often driven by politics or other non-technology or nonbusiness factors.

2. Stress levels can be high due to competition and demanding schedules.

3. Unlike other professions (such as medicine, law, accounting), there is not a well-defined standard/bar for technology professionals. There have been attempts to create such standards (like the PE certification), but none have really succeeded. It is a bit of the Wild West when it comes to who can claim to be an engineer or a technology professional.

STEPHEN NICHOLLS

SENIOR PROJECT MANAGER

ROBERT BOSCH GMBH

Prior Roles: *In the USA: Experimental Services Engineer; New Product Development Manager.*

In Germany: Development Engineer; Project Leader; Project Manager; Customer Project Manager; Global Task Force Leader; Project Manager Original Equipment Sales Europe; Senior Project Manager; Global Project Manager.

Education: *Bachelor of Science—Mechanical Engineering, MIT '92; Master of Science—Ocean Engineering, MIT '93.*

"Luck is what happens when preparation meets opportunity."

— *Seneca (Roman philosopher)*

Better said in Latin in the action movie The Mechanic:

"Amat victoria curam (victory loves preparation)."

How did you narrow down your interest(s) to your specific profession?

Interests, circumstances, and luck led me to my specific profession. High school, career-interest surveys steered me toward engineering. High school and undergraduate course experience (good and bad) steered me toward mechanical engineering. The Undergraduate Research Opportunity Program (UROP) at MIT steered me toward ocean engineering. My first job after MIT at a "medium-sized" tech company was luckily related to my interests and studies. A large German company then bought the US company where I began and offered me the opportunity to transfer to Germany.

When did you first realize that you were interested in your profession? If this occurred during high school, how did you pursue this interest as a high school student?

High school, career-interest surveys showed me that engineering interested me more than other topics. I followed my interests in high school and took extra math and chemistry courses at San

Jose State University and UC Berkeley during the summers.

How did you break into the industry associated with your profession? What advice would you have for a high school student who is interested in breaking into the same industry?

My graduate adviser at MIT led me to an opportunity that was turned down by another graduate student whom he knew. My advice to any university student would be to take advantage of work or research opportunities during your studies to "test out" the field before graduation and to snoop around for future opportunities. If it is a positive experience, great! Then you're heading in the right direction. If it is a negative experience, then also great if you've learned something about what you like or dislike.

What advice would you have for high school students who are interested in a profession that is similar to yours? Is there anything specific that you suggest that these high school students should do?

Strive to be as well-rounded as possible. Good grades in math and science are, of course, important, but people skills will help you excel beyond the laboratory environment later in your career. Skills such as languages and those developed through sports and social activities may prove more important later in life than expected.

What are some aspects of your profession that the average high school student would not know but should know? What are some aspects that surprise you about your profession?

Culture affects behavior and decision-making far more than expected. It is important to be aware of it and adapt. Careers and corporate culture are similar across various industries but rewarded differently and often unfairly.

If you were to hire the ideal job candidate for your profession, what kind of person would you be hiring? What qualities would this person have?

Talented. Open-minded. Able to learn quickly. Honest with oneself and others.

Please list your favorite three aspects of your profession.

Technical challenges. Cultural challenges. Travel opportunities.

Please list your three least-favorite aspects about your profession.

Incompetence. Politics. Inequity.

Please list any additional comments that you have here.

Good luck finding your favorites and defeating stumbling blocks getting in the way.

BRENT STEPHENS

PRINCIPAL

SMISLOVA, KEHNEMUI & ASSOCIATES, P.A. (SK&A)

Prior Roles: I had various summer internships during undergraduate school, including working at Virginia Transportation Research Council in Charlottesville. I was a research assistant during graduate school at the structural materials lab at UT Austin along with working part time for a structural engineering consulting firm during my graduate studies. At SK&A, I was a Structural Engineer, Project Manager, and Associate prior to current position of Principal.

Education: Bachelor of Science in Civil Engineering—University of Virginia; Master of Science in Civil Engineering (with Structural Focus)—University of Texas at Austin.

How did you narrow down your interest(s) to your specific profession?

Coming out of high school, I had such a strong interest in the science and technology subjects that I entered an engineering program for undergraduate studies. I had such an interest in carpentry, construction, and buildings that I gravitated toward civil engineering and, eventually, the specific study of structural engineering while going through undergraduate and graduate studies.

When did you first realize that you were interested in your profession? If this occurred during high school, how did you pursue this interest as a high school student?

Over summers in high school, I volunteered for a program called Salkehatchie that involved helping with repairing or rebuilding homes. I learned a lot about carpentry and other types of construction. When younger, I was very into Legos, Lincoln Logs, etc., so I always liked building things. This background led me to eventually study structural engineering in school.

As a graduate student, I took an elective related to the repair and restoration of existing structures, and I was intrigued by the detective and forensic work needed to evaluate and design repairs to address structure aging and deterioration. I liked the hands-on nature of the work and good mix of time in the office and on jobsites. I performed a part-time job in the field of structural repair consulting while in grad school and determined it was a career path I wanted to pursue.

How did you break into the industry associated with your profession? What advice would you have for a high school student who is interested in breaking into the same industry?

I went to a graduate study program in the specific field I was interested in (structural engineering) to get more detailed coursework and lab/research work. Undergraduate studies in civil engineering cover a broad range of subjects, including transportation, geotechnical, and environmental engineering, in addition to structural engineering, such that you get general knowledge in all civil engineering subjects, while graduate school helps you get expertise in the specific subject you most enjoy. Working a part-time job in private consulting while in graduate school was also a good experience that is a big plus to an employer hiring an entry-level engineer. These steps helped me get to the company I currently work at immediately after completing graduate school.

Based on my experiences, I would recommend a high school student consider graduate school immediately after undergrad if pursuing a verifiably specific field like structural engineering. Students can consider schools that have a BS/MS combined five-year program.

Additionally, gaining work experience through part-time jobs or summer internships in their field of interest is a good way for high school students to confirm it is a job they will enjoy and helps with future employment opportunities.

What advice would you have for high school students who are interested in a profession that is similar to yours? Is there anything specific that you suggest that these high school students should do?

As outlined in the prior question, I would recommend pursuing getting a master's degree in the field to improve employment opportunities and general knowledge of the subject. This requirement may vary by engineering fields, but most require an expertise above the broad knowledge gained during undergraduate studies. Some engineers start work with a bachelor's degree and get their master's later through evening school or online programs while working. Most employers support this effort, for example, by assisting with tuition costs, so that is another path.

Internships or part-time work in the field either during high school, undergrad, or grad school are great ways to learn and improve chances of employment. Joining clubs or becoming student members in organizations related to the profession are also good ways to explore your interest in a subject and get exposure to the industry. Strong organizations in my field include ASCE (American Society of Civil Engineers); ACI (American Concrete Institute); ICRI (International Concrete Repair Institute); etc.

What are some aspects of your profession that the average high school student would not know but should know? What are some aspects that surprise you about your profession?

My specific profession of structural engineering related to repair and restoration of existing structures provides a combination of hands-on field work at jobsites (e.g., performing evaluations, inspections, material testing, etc.) along with the conventional engineering efforts (e.g., performing designs, drafting drawings, running analysis software, etc.) in the office.

The perception of engineering may be that you will be confined to a lab or cubicle with limited interaction with the outside world. This is a profession where there is great variety to each day, with a mix of field and office work and daily interaction and communication with clients, contractors, etc.

If you were to hire the ideal job candidate for your profession, what kind of person would you be hiring? What qualities would this person have?

While having a good technical understanding of the subject is key for a young engineer, communication skills (verbal and written) and work ethic are equally as important.

An eagerness to learn and ask questions, having a good combination of confidence and humility, and big-picture thinking are also important qualities.

Please provide a quote or mantra that you feel accurately reflects both you and your profession. It can be a quote generated by you or a quote from someone else. If the quote or mantra is from someone else, please specify who generated the quote or mantra.

I can't think of a catchy quote off the top of my head, but a general mantra for work and life is achieving a good balance. Balance keeps perspective and helps someone be more successful in all aspects of one's career and other stages of life.

Please list your favorite three aspects of your profession.

The variety keeps each day interesting and challenging, and I always feel like there is something new to learn and be discovered. I enjoy the long-term relationships that come with working with repeat clients, contractors, and colleagues. I enjoy the tangible results of a completed repair project where we can go from surveying a deteriorated structure to seeing a building restored to "as good as new" at the end of the job.

Please list your three least-favorite aspects about your profession.

Like any profession, particularly in the metropolitan Washington, DC, market, the work can be demanding, with short deadlines, off-hour work hours (nights and weekends), and limited margin for error with plenty of competition in the area. These challenges are offset by good life balance, working for a supportive employer that looks out for your well-being, and targeting working with good clients and contractors that promote good teamwork and cooperation in completing projects.

How has your industry changed since the pandemic?

Frankly, the long-term impacts are still TBD as things continue to evolve. That said, we have definitely learned to fine-tune our existing technology and utilize new technology for better virtual communication and to maintain productivity when working from home. Our staff has gotten used to working efficiently from home to the point where many will likely consider at least partially working from home after this pandemic to take advantage of the flexibility and to avoid things like a long commute to work, etc. The impact on individuals' work has varied significantly depending on their personal situations (e.g., young children at home, limitations regarding having an office space at home to work, health concerns, etc.). Long-term changes to the workplace environment and procedures for conducting our work is definitely something our company will constantly be evaluating as we continue to get through these unique times.

LON VAN GELOVEN

FORMER PROCESS ENGINEER OF MANUFACTURING

FORD MOTOR COMPANY

Prior Roles: *(1) Test Engineer at Newport News Shipbuilding, (2) Research Engineer at MIT, (3) Research Engineer at Mercedes-Benz, (4) Research Engineer at Shell, (5) Process Engineer at Ford, and (6) Material Planner at Ford.*

Education: *BSME, MIT (ME = Mechanical Engineering); MSMSE, Stanford (MSE = Manufacturing Systems Engineering).*

"Be creative, energetic, and willing to take on any challenge."

How did you narrow down your interest(s) to your specific profession?

I focused on doing something that I knew I loved: making and fixing things. At home, as a kid, I did a lot of odd jobs around the house and was always involved in some kind of DIY [do-it-yourself] project.

When did you first realize that you were interested in your profession? If this occurred during high school, how did you pursue this interest as a high school student?

In high school, I was good at math and science, so I knew I wanted to do something technical in college. Once I got to college, I took classes in a few different disciplines: computer science, economics, and mechanical engineering. And by sophomore year in college, I knew I wanted to do mechanical engineering.

How did you break into the industry associated with your profession? What advice would you have for a high school student who is interested in breaking into the same industry?

Building up an experience base is important. I did that through (1) projects in college, and (2) summer internships. With an experience base that you can put on your resume, you have a chance to interest people in you and your capability and potential.

What advice would you have for high school students who are interested in a profession that is similar to yours? Is there anything specific that you suggest that these high school students should do?

For engineering, make sure you understand the fundamental concepts in math and science classes in high school. This will help you in your college classes tremendously. Once you understand and can work with the basic building blocks of engineering, then the higher-level subjects will not be mysterious or confusing.

What are some aspects of your profession that the average high school student would not know but should know? What are some aspects that surprise you about your profession?

People skills and leadership skills are just as important as technical skills in engineering. You cannot achieve anything on your own in engineering; you have to be able to work with suppliers, vendors, factory workers, and customers. It's not enough to be a reclusive technical nerd, so, in high school, push yourself into doing things with groups and getting good at working and being with people.

If you were to hire the ideal job candidate for your profession, what kind of person would you be hiring? What qualities would this person have?

Solid grades in college, ideally from a known college. Evidence of achieving some technical projects at college and in summer internships. In an interview, candidates must be able to articulate clearly and efficiently the experiences they have had and the benefits to their work. And then, in an interview, candidates need to be able to think on their feet and answer questions they have never heard before.

Please list your favorite three aspects of your profession.

Being creative, practical, in demand.

Please list your three least-favorite aspects about your profession.

Stress of making production metrics, unhappy or unkind people, working many hours per week.

8 ENTREPRENEURSHIP

SUZIE BERNARD

FORMER SELF-EMPLOYED HORTICULTURIST

Education: École des Métiers de L'horticulture de Montréal.

"Everything becomes simple when you immerse yourself in nature."

— *Mary Reynolds*

How did you narrow down your interest(s) to your specific profession?

I worked in different fields—in a financial institution and in occupational therapy—prior to becoming a horticulturist. After many years away from the labor market, I decided to work in a field that I had really liked for years, one in which I could decide my own schedule.

When did you first realize that you were interested in your profession? If this occurred during high school, how did you pursue this interest as a high school student?

I have liked gardening for a long time, but the interest started long after high school.

How did you break into the industry associated with your profession? What advice would you have for a high school student who is interested in breaking into the same industry?

I have a few clients at a time; all of them generated from word of mouth. I choose them carefully so that I can be completely happy when I am at work. For those who want a larger client base, I would advise placing ads in the local newspaper.

What advice would you have for high school students who are interested in a profession that is similar to yours? Is there anything specific that you suggest that these high school students should do?

It is possible to study through a horticulture program that lasts only one year. Other programs last three years, and the positions that you find after getting a three-year degree may be more interesting and the paycheck may be better.

What are some aspects of your profession that the average high school student would not know but should know? What are some aspects that surprise you about your profession?

Winter is a quiet season, and you may not find a job during those months (depending on the type of work you perform).

If you were to hire the ideal job candidate for your profession, what kind of person would you be hiring? What qualities would this person have?

An early bird, someone in good physical shape, an enthusiast who likes the outdoors, someone who is not afraid to work hard and who has some artistic sense.

Please list your favorite three aspects of your profession.

Doing my own schedule, choosing the projects and the clients, working outdoors, and helping my clients to have beautiful gardens.

Please list your three least-favorite aspects about your profession.

When it is very quiet in winter, working in the cold or on a too-hot or rainy day. The salary is not high, unfortunately (though, if you start your own business, the salary is better).

How has your industry changed since the pandemic?

The nursery where I work opened to the public two weeks later than usual.

Usually, four workers from Mexico come to help for the summer. They did not come this year because the owner of the nursery was not even sure we would open at all. So, now, instead of those experienced workers (the same guys came year after year), we have kids from the village. This probably has not equated to the same efficiency, but it has not mattered.

COVID-19 has seriously affected our line of work because, all of a sudden, everybody wants to build a vegetable garden. Is it because people will not travel this summer, meaning that they can be there to water the garden? Is it because people are worried that the grocery store will not have enough food for everybody? Or is it because what previously was the budget for travel is now spent on shrubs, trees, perennials, and annuals instead? Whatever the reason, at the nursery, sales are much, much higher this year than they were in even our best years. Some days, sales are four to six times higher.

It is nice to see people trying to produce fresh vegetables and fruits. It opens eyes when people try to produce their own fresh vegetables and fruits or buy them locally.

ROHIT BHARGAVA

ENTREPRENEUR, AUTHOR, AND PROFESSIONAL SPEAKER

NON-OBVIOUS COMPANY
[INNOVATIVE ORGANIZATIONAL AND PERSONAL DEVELOPMENT]

Prior Roles: SVP Brand Strategy, Ogilvy;
Executive Producer, Leo Burnett; Waiter, Kramerbooks & Afterwards Cafe

Education: BA, English Literature—Emory University;
BBA, Marketing—Goizueta Business School, Emory University;
MA, English—George Mason University.

"Be Non-Obvious."

How did you narrow down your interest(s) to your specific profession?

I am not sure that I have! My journey has gone from being an "executive producer" for websites (which is basically like a project manager for teams building large sites) to leading brand strategy, to becoming an author and a professional keynote speaker, to finally leaving to start two businesses and be an entrepreneur. Along the way, I also started teaching a university course at Georgetown University. All of these give me a change of pace and let me have passion for different things and use different skills as well.

When did you first realize that you were interested in your profession? If this occurred during high school, how did you pursue this interest as a high school student?

I knew in high school that I was interested in writing and storytelling. In school, that translated into drama and writing plays and screenplays. I even spent a summer interning at a theater.

When I got to college, I wasn't sure what I wanted to study but ended up with English as my main major and studied a lot of poetry. It turned out to be great training for marketing because both require you to be very deliberate with the words you choose.

In high school, though, my interest was limited to English. I never really took any marketing or business classes, and I never learned how to be a speaker on the stage either. Sometimes the things we end up doing aren't directly related to what we did in high school!

How did you break into the industry associated with your profession? What advice would you have for a high school student who is interested in breaking into the same industry?

For me, my big break came when I moved to Australia without a job or knowing anyone there and forcing myself to reinvent a new identity there. I was twenty-three years old and managed to get my first job as a three-week gig coding HTML for front-end websites. The only reason I knew how to do that was because I had gotten a 400-page book a few months earlier called *Teach Yourself HTML in a Week*, and I went through it and taught myself. It was 1998 and that was becoming a pretty marketable skill. So, I took the job offer I had, and it turned into a project manager job, which then helped me to build my network.

What advice would you have for high school students who are interested in a profession that is similar to yours? Is there anything specific that you suggest that these high school students should do?

Become a content creator and try to find your voice. For me, it was through writing, but other people like audio, or drawing, or video. It doesn't really matter what you choose to do, but thinking about creating something and building your skills to do it can really help you to figure out not only what you like, but also what you are good at. Or what you could *become* good at with the right mentor and the right practice.

What are some aspects of your profession that the average high school student would not know but should know? What are some aspects that surprise you about your profession?

When you enter the world of professional services, there are no price tags on items. As a result, you have to determine on your own what you are worth and what you are going to charge. What this means is that many people starting out won't set their price higher because they are unsure about what they should be charging or what they are worth. The variability of pricing is something that surprises a lot of students. There are some professional speakers, for example, that charge $75,000 to deliver a one-hour talk. Others will do it for free because they want to grow their business or get the visibility. The point is, there isn't really ever a "right" price, only what you are able to justify and what you feel right about charging.

If you were to hire the ideal job candidate for your profession, what kind of person would you be hiring? What qualities would this person have?

The type of person I usually look for is someone who puts curiosity above most other things. When you have curiosity, you figure things out. You don't give up easily. You are willing to embrace different points of view, and you are not quick to judge other people or to put limits and restrictions on yourself. A lot of good things start from curiosity.

Please provide a quote or mantra that you feel accurately reflects both you and your profession. It can be a quote generated by you or a quote from someone else. If the quote or mantra is from someone else, please specify who generated the quote or mantra.

"Be Non-Obvious."

Thanks to my many years working in marketing, I definitely like to stay on brand! The reason I like this phrase, though, is because it is a reminder to say things that no one else is saying and see things that everyone else is missing. I believe we can all train ourselves to do that, and, when we do, we can outperform and win because we end up seeing the world more completely and differently than anyone else.

Please list your favorite aspects of your profession.

Time control—Now, as an entrepreneur, I control my own time. If I want to spend the afternoon playing soccer with my boys in the middle of the week, I don't have to ask anyone or pretend like I'm not doing it. Owning how you spend your day is the greatest luxury and benefit of being an entrepreneur.

Impact—As a speaker, I can take the stage for a short period of time and have an outsized impact in how someone thinks. It's not only about me but the fact that they are usually at an event where they are ready to learn something new. As a result, you have this unique opportunity to change how they see the world if you can create a relevant and interesting talk and give them a story. Books are the same way, where you have a chance as an author to create impact in the lives of people whom you have never even met. That impact is a beautiful thing, and it energizes me.

Variety—I work in lots of different industries and travel to many different places, and every day is a different experience. This variety keeps you fresh and helps you to not feel stuck, and I rely on the variety to give me energy.

Please list your least-favorite aspects about your profession.

Evil people—There are far too many speakers or influencers or marketers who use their skills for evil (like doing political advertising or promoting sugary breakfast cereals). I hate that there are so many talented people in my industry who are choosing to use their considerable talents to do things that are quantifiably making the world worse.

Grammar—I am a writer and have published seven books so far. I spend a significant part of my time writing, and I even started a publishing company to help others publish their books. And I secretly despise grammar. My usage of commas sucks, and I often have creative sentence styles that are much closer to how people actually talk than how we are taught to write. It makes me sad to think how much of English that we teach to kids is focused on relatively minor things like grammar, and less on things like telling more engaging stories or just learning to love reading. If it were up to me, those would be the things that English class would be all about.

Additional Comments:

If you want to watch some of my best career advice, you watch a series of career advice I recorded for Georgetown as well as lots more of my videos at www.rohitbhargava.com/speaking.

HARESH BHUNGALIA

CHIEF EXECUTIVE OFFICER

CASEPOINT [LEGAL TECHNOLOGY, E-DISCOVERY PLATFORM]

Prior Roles: Co-Founder—2020 Company, LLC, and Other Various Board and Advisory Roles.

Education: BA in Economics, University of Michigan.

"Work hard, play hard."

"Life is too short not to live. But we have to work hard to live it to the fullest."

How did you narrow down your interest(s) to your specific profession?

I always knew I wanted to own my business. Just never really knew what exactly. I guess the market conditions led to where I ended up. My first business was a professional services firm as that was the thing to do at that time in early 2000. My second business is a legal technology business, as there was a technology gap in the legal field and we saw an opportunity.

When did you first realize that you were interested in your profession? If this occurred during high school, how did you pursue this interest as a high school student?

I did not have clarity as to what I wanted to do in high school. But I did know that I did not want to be a doctor or engineer. However, while I was in high school, I always worked and had side gigs—delivering newspapers, reselling goods, etc.

How did you break into the industry associated with your profession? What advice would you have for a high school student who is interested in breaking into the same industry?

I am able to do what I do because I paid attention to what was going on in the market and where the need was. My advice to high school students would be enjoy high school while learning how to work hard, think critically, and have an open mind.

If you were to hire the ideal job candidate for your profession, what kind of person would you be hiring? What qualities would this person have?

We are looking for someone who has a love of learning, is willing to put in the hours, and has the drive and passion to try new things.

Please list your favorite three aspects of your profession.

I get to work with some really smart people. I'm in an industry that is growing. I love going to work every day.

Please list your three least-favorite aspects about your profession.

Letting someone go. Losing an opportunity to grow the business. Clients that are facing challenges.

TERRY HSIAO

FORMER ENTREPRENEUR

INPHOMATCH
[INTEROPERABLE MESSAGING SERVICES]

Prior Roles: Engineer, Engineering Manager, MBA, Strategic Operations, Starting a Company, Raising Capital, Managing Growth, Selling a Company.

Education: Rutgers BSEE in Electrical and Computer Engineering; Master's in Management of Technology, MIT Sloan School of Management.

"A journey of ten thousand miles starts with a single step."

— Chinese Proverb

How did you narrow down your interest(s) to your specific profession?

Once I chose the major in college, it naturally led to an engineering position upon graduation (initially). Then I realized engineering on its own is not too exciting, so I moved to business and management.

When did you first realize that you were interested in your profession? If this occurred during high school, how did you pursue this interest as a high school student?

I was good at math and science, and, as an immigrant, engineering was an easier path than other majors.

How did you break into the industry associated with your profession? What advice would you have for a high school student who is interested in breaking into the same industry?

If students are interested in engineering or STEM in general, I would suggest taking the most challenging math and science classes. Learn about computer science, for example.

What advice would you have for high school students who are interested in a profession that is similar to yours? Is there anything specific that you suggest that these high school students should do?

To be an entrepreneur in high tech, I would challenge high school students to think about how things you come across in life could be done better. Be hands on in designing and building things. Learn how to solve problems with limited resources and information.

What are some aspects of your profession that the average high school student would not know but should know? What are some aspects that surprise you about your profession?

Life is full of ups and downs. Don't ever give up on yourself; things will work themselves out if you keep trying.

If you were to hire the ideal job candidate for your profession, what kind of person would you be hiring? What qualities would this person have?

This person should be curious, hardworking, persistent, and always willing to share information.

Please list your favorite three aspects of your profession.

Resourcefulness, perseverance, excitement.

Please list your three least-favorite aspects about your

Stress, loneliness, raising capital.

Additional Comments:

Having a positive attitude is key.

VIRESH PRASHAR

SOCIAL ENTREPRENEUR

FRUITFAL [HELPING SMALLHOLDER FARMERS USE
TECHNOLOGY FOR A BETTER TOMORROW]

Prior Roles: *Consultant, Director Business Development,
Practice Director, CEO/Co-Founder, Principal Engineer.*

Education: *BSEE—George Mason University;
MSEE—Johns Hopkins University;
MBA—IESE Barcelona.*

*"Imagination is more
important than knowledge."*

— *Albert Einstein*

*"The best way to predict the
future is to create it."*

— *Abraham Lincoln*

"Act. Learn. Build. Repeat."

— *Probably an Ever-Successful Entrepreneur*

How did you narrow down your interest(s) to your specific profession?

From early on I had an interest in understanding how things work. This led me to math/science, where I found I had some affinity, probably driven by the first point. I don't think it was a direct connection to my current profession. I had interests in these subjects and followed them to wherever they went, through exploration, reading, and continued discovery.

I did not really have "profession" on the brain at that time. Just chased things that I thought were cool and interesting.

Lots of subscriptions to *Popular Science*-type magazines, etc....

When did you first realize that you were interested in your profession? If this occurred during high school, how did you pursue this interest as a high school student?

Interestingly, it was two teachers in high school (biology and chemistry) who stimulated my interest in discovering and understanding more about how things work. They were both very encouraging and supported my curiosity, which I think led to me doing well in these subjects, which then prompted even more interest. A nice virtuous circle, if you will.

As a kid, I also spent a lot of time dismantling anything that was held together by a screw to see what was inside—old-style clock radios that had those numbers that would turn over every minute, game machines, watches, toys, portable radios, the lawn mower (Dad was not pleased)—and to see how tuning worked, stuck a pair of tweezers into an electrical socket (Dad *really* not pleased), etc.

How did you break into the industry associated with your profession? What advice would you have for a high school student who is interested in breaking into the same industry?

I would advise students to follow interests and passions first, not industries or professions. Look for things that stimulate you. Things you get so lost in doing that hours/days pass without noticing and things where you create aha/wow moments along the way.

Particularly today when there are so many different outlets/tools/places to be creative and to explore ideas. I think this part is really important: develop imagination and outlets for creativity in whichever form. Explore, experiment, try everything possible (at least once), be open to being led, follow interests to wherever they may go, and

just see what happens. Let the industry, profession, title, money, etc. come after (which it will, if you follow the first bit of advice).

What advice would you have for high school students who are interested in a profession that is similar to yours? Is there anything specific that you suggest that these high school students should do?

I am now in an "industry" of using technology for social good—i.e., development of a for-profit business that has outcomes of social impact. In my case, it is to help smallholder farmers in India improve their incomes by providing direct linkages to markets using smartphones, connectivity, data science, and other technology.

It would have been impossible for me to have known in high school what to do to now be working on the project that I am. The advice I would give here is similar to the advice provided earlier—follow and develop interests.

Discover things in which you get lost—tinkering, playing, dancing, singing, creating—no matter how crazy or wild. Cultivate imagination and curiosity and look for purpose in what you do.

What are some aspects of your profession that the average high school student would not know but should know? What are some aspects that surprise you about your profession?

Technology can be used to help people and improve the lives of others—not just for more photo-sharing and chatting (although those things are fun). As technology advances and becomes more and more accessible to people around the world, it can be used as a vehicle.

The one thing that has surprised me is the number of people who are interested in helping others and looking for purpose in what they do. While I am relatively new and a novice to the whole area of social entrepreneurship, I am discovering very motivated groups of people (and funding sources) using technology and innovation to have an impact on important social causes, like agriculture, education, health, sanitation, financial, and digital inclusion, etc.

The usual suspects, of course, are still here—e.g., the World Bank and other development agencies who are involved in traditional support of development projects—but I was very surprised to discover the large number of start-ups in the space (supported by venture capital firms funding innovation) that tackle these challenging issues.

If you were to hire the ideal job candidate for your profession, what kind of person would you be hiring? What qualities would this person have?

I would hire someone who has demonstrated himself or herself to be intensely curious, who has been motivated to try many things, and who has learned something from each experience to bring to the next. Someone who has imagination and is not afraid to try regardless of the outcome.

Please list your favorite three aspects of your profession.

Something new to learn and discover every day. Motivated people working hard to make lives better for people. Huge opportunity to develop creative solutions for very challenging problems.

Please list your three least-favorite aspects about your profession.

Social entrepreneur—sometimes still very hard to convince people that "doing good" can be profitable. Not enough technology, energy, and expertise being applied to make a real difference. Not enough funding sources for impact projects.

Additional Comments:

A bit cliché—but chase what you are passionate about. Doesn't really matter what, but explore and find things you like and are good at. Develop those interests. Experiment. Try. Fail. Learn. Try again. Play. Have fun.

Get involved in all kinds of activities. Take lessons. Learn how to do "stuff." Meet people. Learn from them. Connect the dots. Create new things. Don't focus so much on industry or profession or career. That stuff will come.

9 EVENT PLANNING

ASHLEY BERKERY

OWNER

ASHLEY COPELAND INC.

Prior Roles: French Teacher and Newspaper Editor.

Education: Auburn University—Double Major Communications and French; University of Alabama Birmingham (UAB)—Master of French Education.

"Do it right the first time."

How did you narrow down your interest(s) to your specific profession?

I've always loved coordinating and planning events!

When did you first realize that you were interested in your profession? If this occurred during high school, how did you pursue this interest as a high school student?

It really happened in college when I took an interest in planning sorority events and then trips to France for my French students when I was a teacher. In high school, I was just really organized, which led me to like event planning.

How did you break into the industry associated with your profession? What advice would you have for a high school student who is interested in breaking into the same industry?

I broke into the industry by meeting with wedding vendors, picking their brains, and asking for referrals.

What advice would you have for high school students who are interested in a profession that is similar to yours? Is there anything specific that you suggest that these high school students should do?

Reach out to all vendors in your category, introduce yourself, and ask if you can shadow them.

What are some aspects of your profession that the average high school student would not know but should know? What are some aspects that surprise you about your profession?

People are all different, so make sure your "plan" fits each client individually.

If you were to hire the ideal job candidate for your profession, what kind of person would you be hiring? What qualities would this person have?

A very organized and personable individual.

Please list your favorite three aspects of your profession.

A happy client, finding the right vendors for my client, satisfaction at the end of the event.

Please list your three least-favorite aspects about your profession.

A needy bride/client, a distrustful client, working a twelve-hour wedding day on my feet.

JULIE LANZA

SPECIAL PROJECTS COORDINATOR

WELLESLEY COLLEGE

Prior Roles: Content Editor, Harcourt.com; Senior Project Editor, Houghton Mifflin; Production Editor, DC Heath; Editorial Assistant, Houghton Mifflin.

Education: Wellesley College, BA; Boston University, MEd.

"Perfection is not attainable, but if we chase perfection, we can catch excellence."

— Vince Lombardi

How did you narrow down your interest(s) to your specific profession?

My career path has undergone a big shift since I took time out of the workforce to raise my three daughters. During college, I majored in English and Spanish and realized that I wanted to work in a field related to my love of literature and interest in education. I worked for thirteen years in educational publishing, took over ten years off to raise my family, and now I am working part time at my alma mater in a position that involves event management. My current job is a big change from my publishing career, but many of the necessary skill sets are the same.

When did you first realize that you were interested in your profession? If this occurred during high school, how did you pursue this interest as a high school student?

I did not have a clear sense of what profession I wanted to pursue during high school. I had always loved books, but I did not do any career exploration until college. During college, I did an internship with an author who was working on a book about buying art at auctions. I really enjoyed that experience and it sparked my interest in a publishing career.

While I was working in publishing, I had always thought that it would be an ideal profession for working parents, as publishers often hire freelancers for many of their projects. When I first started working again when my children were older, I accepted some freelance jobs, but it was not as reliable or flexible as I had hoped, and I missed working at an office with a community of coworkers. I decided to look for a part-time job, with "mother's hours" and flexibility. I had to expand my search beyond the publishing world. I was very fortunate to find my position at Wellesley College. While my career path no longer involves publishing, I am still working in the field of education, in an environment that values learning, and provides a lot of flexibility for me as a parent.

How did you break into the industry associated with your profession? What advice would you have for a high school student who is interested in breaking into the same industry?

Regardless of what industry you are looking into, I think trying to find an internship is an invaluable experience. If it gives you even a small glimpse into that profession, you will be better informed. An internship experience might give you contacts that will help you find a job in the future. It might help you narrow down your search, or it might give you new ideas about what parts of the industry do (or don't!) appeal to you.

What advice would you have for high school students who are interested in a profession that is similar to yours? Is there anything specific that you suggest that these high school students should do?

As I said in my previous answer, I think that an internship can be a very rewarding experience, both for building your resume and allowing you to reflect on how the industry/profession you were exploring fits with your interests and goals.

If you are interested in publishing, you should read, read, read. Also, being involved in school literary journals or newspapers would give you some relevant experience. If you are interested in event management, then you could volunteer to help school organizations, charitable organizations, or political organizations with their events.

What are some aspects of your profession that the average high school student would not know but should know? What are some aspects that surprise you about your profession?

Event planning can involve some very long hours and some stressful moments, and much of the work is not very glamorous. Behind every event, there is a team working together on all the details to pull it off. I really like the teamwork involved in event planning, and I find the job rewarding because the events and programs are valued by students and the college community.

If you were to hire the ideal job candidate for your profession, what kind of person would you be hiring? What qualities would this person have?

In my current position in events management, the ideal candidate should be very organized, detail-oriented, and a problem-solver, as well as able to plan, anticipate, and take initiative. A positive attitude is also key, as is the ability to work well with lots of different personalities. As I said before, most of these skill sets also apply to candidates looking to be successful in publishing.

Please provide a quote or mantra that you feel accurately reflects both you and your profession. It can be a quote generated by you or a quote from someone else.

I don't really have a mantra that I turn to, but I do like this Vince Lombardi quote: "Perfection is not attainable, but if we chase perfection, we can catch excellence."

I think it relates to my job now because in event planning, you need to do the best you can, realize that something will not go as planned, and be able to adapt and move on to make the event the best you can.

Please list your favorite aspects of your profession.

1. I like to work with students and feel like I am contributing to their experiences and learning.
2. I like the teamwork involved in pulling together a good program or event.
3. At this point in my career, I am very grateful to have found a job and employer that will support my need to work part time.

Please list your least-favorite aspects about your profession.

1. Stress always peaks right before the event begins.
2. With the increased prevalence of food allergies, planning a menu for large events that involve food has become really tricky and challenging.

10 GOVERNMENT, POLITICS, & POLITICAL AFFAIRS

JAMES PHILLIP BATTEY

FORMER SENIOR VICE PRESIDENT OF EXTERNAL AFFAIRS

INTRAFI NETWORK

Prior Roles: Washington Correspondent, American Banker Newspaper; Director of Editorial Services, American Bankers Association; Speechwriter to the Comptroller of the Currency and the Chairman of the Federal Deposit Insurance Corporation; Director, External Affairs, Federal Deposit Insurance Corporation.

Education: Bachelor of Science in Foreign Service, Georgetown University; Master of Arts (Journalism), University of Missouri—Columbia.

"Never complain; never explain."

— Benjamin Disraeli

How did you narrow down your interest(s) to your specific profession?

I wanted to work in Washington, DC, in an area that would cover what was once called "communications," business, and politics.

When did you first realize that you were interested in your profession? If this occurred during high school, how did you pursue this interest as a high school student?

The profession enables me to work where the three interests expressed above [communications, business, and politics] meet.

I didn't develop my strategic plan until after college and then had to get a graduate degree in journalism and serve apprenticeships as a reporter and speechwriter to develop the knowledge and skills to make it happen.

How did you break into the industry associated with your profession? What advice would you have for a high school student who is interested in breaking into the same industry?

If the "breaking into" is my initial job as a newspaper reporter, I would tell a high school student to forget about it—the industry is dying, so there is no future in it. If we are looking at "breaking into" external affairs in Washington, DC, I would advise going to law school after college but with the intent of never practicing law.

What advice would you have for high school students who are interested in a profession that is similar to yours? Is there anything specific that you suggest that these high school students should do?

In college, take an accounting course or two and three or four economics courses. Then major in something you enjoy and that will give you some background to work from: history, political science, etc. Don't major in English, but do learn to write.

What are some aspects of your profession that the average high school student would not know but should know? What are some aspects that surprise you about your profession?

I've been working in Washington's "banking village" for forty years. All of us know—or know of—each other. The biggest professional compliment I ever received was from a banking lobbyist who once said to me that all the banking lobbyists in town trusted me (I was working for the head of a government agency at the time) because I had never lied or misled anyone.

You're going to be working for a long time, and a reputation for honesty and integrity is as important as anything else you bring to your job.

The biggest surprise in doing what I do is that I still work with people whom I worked with thirty-five years ago. The second biggest is that the people I have worked for have mostly been exceptional in one way or the other.

If you were to hire the ideal job candidate for your profession, what kind of person would you be hiring? What qualities would this person have?

Someone who can write well, speak well, learn quickly, and keep confidences.

What are your favorite and least-favorite parts about your profession?

Favorite parts—In my last role, I was well-compensated. I worked with people whom I liked and had faith in, and that was mostly the case at my previous jobs. I had some great experiences as a senior federal official because I reported directly to—and worked directly with—the heads of agencies.

Least-favorite—Talking with reporters. It is always a crapshoot.

PAUL WEINSTEIN

FORMER SPECIAL ASSISTANT TO THE PRESIDENT AND FORMER CHIEF OF STAFF OF THE WHITE HOUSE DOMESTIC POLICY COUNCIL

THE WHITE HOUSE CLINTON-GORE ADMINISTRATION

Prior Roles: *Legislative Assistant—Senator Albert Gore, Senior; Legislative Assistant— Representative C. Thomas McMillen; Associate Issues Director—Gore for President 1988; Fellow, Progressive Policy Institute; Senior Adviser, Policy Department—Clinton-Gore for President 1992; Senior Adviser—1992 Office of the Presidential Transition; Senior Policy Analyst—Domestic Policy Council, the White House.*

Education: *Bachelor of Science in Foreign Service, Georgetown University; Master of Arts, Columbia University; University of Maryland, Doctoral Program in Government (not finished).*

How did you narrow down your interest(s) to your specific profession?

I have always had a strong interest in government and history. After interviewing with several Wall Street firms following graduate school, I decided instead to go work on Al Gore's presidential campaign in 1988.

When did you first realize that you were interested in your profession? If this occurred during high school, how did you pursue this interest as a high school student?

As noted above, I always had a strong interest in government and public service. There was not a lot of opportunity in high school to pursue this interest outside of reading extensively about the field. However, I did do an internship for my local

congressman between my sophomore and junior year of high school.

How did you break into the industry associated with your profession? What advice would you have for a high school student who is interested in breaking into the same industry?

Unlike other sectors, there is no clear path into government and politics.

I was mainly interested in national policy issues, so I was most interested in working for a president. That is not easy and it involves some luck (as in your candidate has to win). Even though I had a graduate degree, I initially had to volunteer with the Gore campaign in 1988 before I got a paid position. It is a struggle, there is little money in the beginning, and the hours are long. But it is a lot of fun and can be very rewarding.

What advice would you have for high school students who are interested in a profession that is similar to yours? Is there anything specific that you suggest that these high school students should do?

Hone your writing skills. It is the key to success at this level.

What are some aspects of your profession that the average high school student would not know but should know? What are some aspects that surprise you about your profession?

Government, particularly at the higher levels, can actually be somewhat entrepreneurial. Yes, there is bureaucracy, but there is also the opportunity to be creative when working on new policies or changes to existing programs.

If you were to hire the ideal job candidate for your profession, what kind of person would you be hiring? What qualities would this person have?

Common sense, hardworking, good writer, data skills.

Please list your favorite three aspects of your profession.

Creativity. Public service. Challenge.

Please list your three least-favorite aspects about your profession.

Bureaucracy. Hyper-partisanship. Having to watch your back all the time.

11 HEALTH CARE & MEDICINE

CHARLIE CHOI

CHIEF EXECUTIVE OFFICER

AXIA WOMEN'S HEALTH

Prior Roles: Group VP, Avanti Group and Lab, DaVita; Division VP, Woodlands Division, DaVita; VP, Hospital Supply Category Management, Cardinal Health; Junior Partner, McKinsey; Engineering Team Leader, Ford.

Education: MBA and MS Manufacturing Engineering, University of Michigan; BS Mechanical Engineering, MIT.

"Help people do what they love and love what they do."

How did you narrow down your interest(s) to your specific profession?

I started as an engineer and enjoyed the team leadership and strategy aspects of the job, but not the technical aspects. My MBA helped me understand business strategy, and leadership represented a better career fit. McKinsey consulting helped me explore many industries and functions to realize I was most interested in general management in health care. Cardinal Health confirmed my interest in general management; DaVita narrowed that interest to health care services.

When did you first realize that you were interested in your profession? If this occurred during high school, how did you pursue this interest as a high school student?

Didn't realize until seventeen years after high school!

How did you break into the industry associated with your profession? What advice would you have for a high school student who is interested in breaking into the same industry?

Exposure through consulting helped me to land a senior strategy role in health care, which I used to gain visibility with top management to land a general-management role.

What advice would you have for high school students who are interested in a profession that is similar to yours? Is there anything specific that you suggest that these high school students should do?

Pick something and try it; don't stress too much about picking the wrong thing. You will learn something and can always switch. If you're interested in becoming a CEO or taking on another leadership role within health care, there are many ways to start exploring. My advice would be to take initiative in school, be a leader, and follow one or two passions, rather than spreading yourself too thin just to build your resume.

What are some aspects of your profession that the average high school student would not know but should know? What are some aspects that surprise you about your profession?

The most important skill needed is connecting with people at a human level, caring about them, revealing who you really are, and being genuinely interested in helping them.

If you were to hire the ideal job candidate for your profession, what kind of person would you be hiring? What qualities would this person have?

Leadership and initiative.

Please list your favorite three aspects of your profession.

Helping people grow. Building a business that makes the world better. Creating a culture of community.

Please list your three least-favorite aspects about your profession.

Managing limited cash. Having to fire people, especially people I like but who are just in the wrong job. Writing reports.

Additional Comments:

I hope you do what you love and love what you do.

DR. MOIRA SHANAHAN

OBSTETRICIAN - GYNECOLOGIST

DARTMOUTH-HITCHCOCK MEDICAL CENTER

Prior Roles: I worked in a hospital-owned group practice providing outpatient care to women, obstetric management for vaginal birth or cesarean section, and gynecology care, including surgery, such as hysterectomy.

Education: BA, Chemistry, Wellesley College; MD, Dartmouth Medical School.

"Primum non nocere (First, do no harm)."

— *Hippocratic Oath*

How did you narrow down your interest(s) to your specific profession?

I wanted a profession that would provide lifelong interest and make use of my interest in science. In high school, I spent several weeks volunteering with a cardiac surgeon. I was able to see surgery but also see his patient interactions and meetings with colleagues. So I was pretty sure when I went to college that I wanted to be a doctor. During medical school, I had courses (rotations) with many different specialties, and ob-gyn was the best fit because it included medical management and surgery.

When did you first realize that you were interested in your profession? If this occurred during high school, how did you pursue this interest as a high school student?

See previous. In high school, I volunteered with a cardiac surgeon. Between high school and college, I worked with a plastic surgeon who was doing reconstructive surgery for children. In both cases, I spent the entire day with the doctor. I was able to see surgery, observe doctors in the office with patients, and participate in meetings among physicians about patient management.

How did you break into the industry associated with your profession? What advice would you have for a high school student who is interested in breaking into the same industry?

Both of the surgeons were parents of fellow high school students. However, I was not friends with either of the high school students. I just sent a letter and a resume to all of the physicians that had children in my high school and started calling around. I think using this connection allowed me to see more than I would have as a regular hospital volunteer. I think another way to seek out opportunity would be to find physicians who are already teaching at medical schools and see if there is a way to participate in their research.

What advice would you have for high school students who are interested in a profession that is similar to yours? Is there anything specific that you suggest that these high school students should do?

I don't think high school students interested in medicine need to have particular activities or courses. However, I do think that it is a good idea to get a "taste" of medical research and an opportunity to shadow a doctor in day-to-day practice in order to figure out if you think you might like this.

What are some aspects of your profession that the average high school student would not know but should know? What are some aspects that surprise you about your profession?

Medicine requires one to work hard, particularly in one's twenties, when many others are spending time building a social network or having a family. Medicine can bring significant educational debt, unless one's family can pay for medical education.

This debt can be repaid, but the process of debt repayment may influence one's choice of specialty or where to practice.

Medicine is never boring, and always useful. It is also incredibly intimate, since I am talking with patients about very personal details of their lives. Given the intimacy of patient care and the constant intellectual challenge, medicine provides something that many other fields do not.

If you were to hire the ideal job candidate for your profession, what kind of person would you be hiring? What qualities would this person have?

Physicians need compassion and persistence. If one is compassionate, then one will be motivated to care for people who are very different from oneself. That motivation and persistence means being willing to look up information when the answer isn't clear, or being willing to get up at 2 a.m. and help someone when needed. Although an interest in science helped me, it is not essential, and hard work is the primary ingredient of a good physician.

Please provide a quote or mantra that you feel accurately reflects both you and your profession. It can be a quote generated by you or a quote from someone else. If the quote or mantra is from someone else, please specify who generated the quote or mantra.

"Primum non nocere."

Primum non nocere means "First, do no harm." This phase is generally part of the Hippocratic oath. It is easy to harm patients by too little intervention, too much intervention, or unkind words or actions. It seems like fulfilling this should be easy, but it isn't.

Please list your favorite three aspects of your profession.

1. Interacting with patients.
2. Learning new information and evaluating scientific data all the time.
3. Making a reliable income, with excellent mobility.

Please list your three least-favorite aspects about your profession.

1. Worrying about patient outcomes can be stressful.
2. My particular specialty involves extensive night work, which is physically tiring.
3. Due to privacy concerns, I can't discuss many aspects of my work with my friends.

Please list any additional comments that you have here.

Medicine is a great field, and there is room for a wide variety of personalities. It is definitely worth considering in high school if students have any interest. It is not essential to determine one's interest then, but it is easier to complete all the requirements if one knows about one's interest when entering college.

DR. LIZHEN WANG

PEDIATRICIAN

VA ALLERGY & PEDIATRICS

Education: Shanghai Jiaotong University Medical School, Shanghai, China.

"Primum non nocere (First, do no harm)."

— *Hippocratic Oath*

When did you first realize that you were interested in your profession? If this occurred during high school, how did you pursue this interest as a high school student?

When I was growing up in China, one of my favorite chores was to clean the chicken and duck corpses. To most people, it sounded gross, but to me it was fascinating. I studied their anatomies and performed surgeries (of course, the destructive ones).

How did you break into the industry associated with your profession? What advice would you have for a high school student who is interested in breaking into the same industry?

During medical school training, every student has to rotate through different departments. I chose pediatrics because I love kids.

What advice would you have for high school students who are interested in a profession that is similar to yours? Is there anything specific that you suggest that these high school students should do?

Study biology and chemistry. Be handy if you want to be a surgeon. Be a good writer and communicator.

What are some aspects of your profession that the average high school student would not know but should know? What are some aspects that surprise you about your profession?

Work for long hours. Constant worry about patients if they do not do well. High debt.

If you were to hire the ideal job candidate for your profession, what kind of person would you be hiring? What qualities would this person have?

Solid knowledge. Willing to work extra hours. Excellent communicator.

Please provide a quote or mantra that you feel accurately reflects both you and your profession. It can be a quote generated by you or a quote from someone else. If the quote or mantra is from someone else, please specify who generated the quote or mantra.

"Primum non nocere."

First to do no harm. It is the Hippocratic oath for all medical students to learn and remember. It reminds physicians to consider the possible harm that any intervention might do.

Please list your favorite three aspects of your profession.

Making patients feel better. Helping family and friends with my medical knowledge.

The most rewarding experience is to watch my patients grow from newborns to adults, to listen to their life stories, to help them to go through struggles, and to share their happiness.

Please list your three least-favorite aspects about your profession.

Giving shots. Getting peed on, vomited on, and covered in saliva and mucus from babies. Waking up at night for emergency phone calls.

CAROL WASMUCKY

OWNER AND PHYSICAL THERAPIST

PET REHAB

Prior Roles: *Staff Physical Therapist, Director of INOVA Outpatient Rehab.*

Education: *BS in PT from the University of Miami.*

"This is the BEST JOB EVER!"

How did you narrow down your interest(s) to your specific profession?

I was a student athletic trainer while in college, studying mechanical engineering—combined the two backgrounds, and went to PT [physical therapy] school. After ten years working on people, my first dog had mild hip dysplasia, and I wanted to do something for him, but there was no such thing as therapy for dogs. So, I started it and took some courses on animals. Friends had injured dogs, and I treated them as I would treat my people patients.

How did you break into the industry associated with your profession? What advice would you have for a high school student who is interested in breaking into the same industry?

After I realized I wanted to rehab animals, I petitioned the Board of Medicine to see if I could actually treat animals. They agreed. I marketed myself to veterinarians in the Northern Virginia area.

What advice would you have for high school students who are interested in a profession that is similar to yours? Is there anything specific that you suggest that these high school students should do?

I would get a PT degree, which you need to treat animals. Some states do not allow you to treat animals, so you would need to look at the practice acts. And if you are unable to treat animals in a state, you could always fall back and treat humans.

What are some aspects of your profession that the average high school student would not know but should know? What are some aspects that surprise you about your profession?

They would not know there is such a field. You need to be a vet, vet tech, PT, or PTA [physical therapist assistant] to treat animals.

If you were to hire the ideal job candidate for your profession, what kind of person would you be hiring? What qualities would this person have?

Must be a PT or PTA. Lots of energy, and must love animals.

What are your favorite and least-favorite parts about your profession?

Love working with the pets, hate the paperwork.

DR. ROBERT WOOD

PROFESSOR OF PEDIATRICS AND DIRECTOR OF PEDIATRIC ALLERGY AND IMMUNOLOGY

THE JOHNS HOPKINS UNIVERSITY SCHOOL OF MEDICINE

Prior Roles: Pediatrician, Pediatric Allergist.

Education: BA, University of Buffalo; MD, University of Rochester School of Medicine.

How did you narrow down your interest(s) to your specific profession?

It was an easy choice to become a doctor. The specific area became clear in medical school.

When did you first realize that you were interested in your profession? If this occurred during high school, how did you pursue this interest as a high school student?

I knew this by fifth grade, probably earlier. I worked as an assistant in our local hospital in high school.

How did you break into the industry associated with your profession? What advice would you have for a high school student who is interested in breaking into the same industry?

There is a very structured path of undergraduate and medical school, followed by training in pediatrics and then subspecialty training.

What advice would you have for high school students who are interested in a profession that is similar to yours? Is there anything specific that you suggest that these high school students should do?

You have to achieve good grades all the way through high school and college. Other than that, you should do what you enjoy.

What are some aspects of your profession that the average high school student would not know but should know? What are some aspects that surprise you about your profession?

It is important to know that you have to work hard and that you will need a minimum of eleven years after high school to actually practice medicine. For some specialties, it can take up to twenty years of school and training.

If you were to hire the ideal job candidate for your profession, what kind of person would you be hiring? What qualities would this person have?

Smart, kind, compassionate, hardworking, honest, and reliable.

Please list your favorite three aspects of your profession.

Patient care. Teaching. Research.

Please list your three least-favorite aspects about your profession.

Paperwork. Insurance companies. Government control over more aspects of health care.

12 IT / TECHNOLOGY

*See the following interviews that relate
to IT / Technology:*

JON BERKERY

HEALTH INSURANCE
SOFTWARE DEVELOPER MANAGER

BLUE CROSS AND BLUE SHIELD OF ALABAMA

Prior Roles: Before my current position, I was a software developer.

Education: Bachelor's Degree—Computer Science; Master's Degree—Business Administration.

"Be Prepared."

— *Boy Scout motto*

"Improvise, Adapt, Overcome."

— Heartbreak Ridge

"Beginnings are scary, endings are sad; it is what you do in the middle that counts."

— *The movie* Hope Floats

How did you narrow down your interest(s) to your specific profession?

I really didn't choose to enter software development. During college, I enrolled in a computer programming class by chance. I excelled in the class, and the skills needed in the course seemed natural to me. Because of that success, I continued with the computer science curriculum. As I progressed, some of those courses were more difficult, such as compiler design, calculus, and operating system design. After completion of the entire curriculum, I realized that I was better suited for the software development side of IT work, and, therefore, I searched for software development opportunities (internships and entry-level jobs).

When did you first realize that you were interested in your profession? If this occurred during high school, how did you pursue this interest as a high school student?

I realized I had an ability for software development in college. Understanding that, I selected computer science as my major and began to take more classes in order to increase my knowledge on the topic. For a high school student, I would suggest the same approach.

If you are aware of a subject that you are good at, continue in that study by selecting electives and other opportunities that expose you to more of that subject.

How did you break into the industry associated with your profession? What advice would you have for a high school student who is interested in breaking into the same industry?

I broke into the industry as a result of my personal network. I was interviewed for both my internship and current job as a result of family members knowing someone at the hiring companies. However, getting hired was the result of my performance in the interview, convincing the interviewers that I was capable, knowledgeable, willing to learn, and a responsible person. What I mean by this is that while my personal network got me an opportunity to talk to the company, I had to convince the company I was the right person for them on my own.

If you were to hire the ideal job candidate for your profession, what kind of person would you be hiring? What qualities would this person have?

In my opinion, the ideal candidate should be reliable (do what you say you are going to do); organized (know what tasks you have to do); communicate well (share your knowledge and the status of your tasks); and willing to research and learn.

Additional Comments:

My best advice would be to identify your natural skills, look for classes that develop those skills, search for opportunities that use those skills, give those opportunities a try, and be prepared for those opportunities to show you new experiences.

When you reflect on that whole process, where you started and where you ended may be totally different … and that is okay.

TOM BURKET

SENIOR DEVELOPMENT MANAGER

CONDUENT

Prior Roles: Software developer, systems engineer, and system architect as a technical contributor, with team leadership and management positions, too. These positions were in commercial product development, research, and federal contracting, including classified work.

Education: BS Computer Science and MS Computer Science, University of Illinois.

"Be someone who gets things done."

How did you narrow down your interest(s) to your specific profession?

In my youth, computers were rare, and even basic electronic calculators were just coming out late in my high school career. Therefore, it was not possible to have experience in "computer science" prior to college, unlike today, when aspects of the field are open to very young students open to self-study. I started out headed to a career in math, physical science, or engineering, but classes in various fields and an assessment of my particular strengths and interests prompted me to select starting my career in computer programming. Perhaps it mattered somewhat that jobs were plentiful. I also felt that programming could lead to many future paths as computers became more pervasive.

When did you first realize that you were interested in your profession? If this occurred during high school, how did you pursue this interest as a high school student?

Because access to computers did not really exist in my high school years—see the origin story of Microsoft for how rare that access was—the software profession was effectively unknown.

We knew computers were out there at some level, such as on the space program, but nobody I ever knew growing up was remotely close to the field. Thus, in my high school years, it was more what is now known as STEM, with the image of the scientist in his lab coat or some generic engineer. My high school was in a rural community where not many went to college, so there was little momentum or shared energy toward a STEM future. It took college to open up possibilities.

How did you break into the industry associated with your profession? What advice would you have for a high school student who is interested in breaking into the same industry?

During college, I thought an advanced degree in computer science would be helpful and decided to go straight through and get the degree. I also had a semester-long internship at a national lab, exposed to adults in the field. I doubted my ability to get that advanced degree later, and that extra time was very helpful to expand my knowledge and readiness, as it included hands-on work with a project team. I built a strong academic record and entered the industry through normal on-campus recruiting by IBM, my first employer. IBM was an elite employer at the time, and Illinois's program was considered among the very best (and still is), so direct recruiting was facilitated.

What advice would you have for high school students who are interested in a profession that is similar to yours? Is there anything specific that you suggest that these high school students should do?

The computer field is incredibly wide now, and it is exceptionally open to self-motivated youth who can learn some on their own and build things. This is not possible in so many other professional fields, such as law and medicine.

I urge students who might be interested in computing to try, if they haven't done so already, making web pages, apps, games, etc. Keep in mind, however, that the computer science field is far more

than just programming. There is a deep technical rigor in many areas. A person can be a successful programmer without deep, rigorous knowledge.

To be a specialist or someone working on large system design, imagine what is behind the scenes at Amazon.com, for example—the field can be a good one for people who want to work on large, complex systems that affect a lot of people.

What are some aspects of your profession that the average high school student would not know but should know? What are some aspects that surprise you about your profession?

Never underestimate the need to work well with others. The potential stereotype of techies silently working off in the corner is not true, although there is room for the highly introverted types, with an understanding that advancement will be difficult.

Working effectively as a team is essential. I have been on some highly successful teams and some completely dysfunctional teams.

No matter how smart and talented you think you are, there are other people with a different perspective or just different ideas. Learn to fit in to that culture. Don't treat everything as a personal competition.

Also, computing is for people with attention to detail. Tiny mistakes can have significant consequences.

Some people can be successful as an "idea guy" who conceptualizes systems or is a "big picture" person, without being much on the details. Those people can be exceptionally valuable, if they survive the more junior positions and if hired into a regular, professional position.

If you were to hire the ideal job candidate for your profession, what kind of person would you be hiring? What qualities would this person have?

I am partial toward smart people who have demonstrated an ability to learn and perform complicated tasks. Ideally, the person has shown some passion for the field, whether the candidate started early or had some fairly recent awakening and switched fields.

If you want to enter the profession because you are looking for a job that pays well, that's not good (if I can figure that out in my assessment). Can you communicate well? I am highly disappointed in the poor quality of writing by so many people during my career, despite its importance. That's hard to assess among fresh candidates. Are you a problem-solver? Can you think in algorithms? Can you work with other cultures?

Please list your favorite three aspects of your profession.

1. Potential to work on real systems that affect real people in a visible way.

2. Potential to work on projects that are essential and primary to the employer.

3. The field is still growing, with many opportunities. If I were starting over, there are so many different areas of possible focus.

Please list your three least-favorite aspects about your profession.

1. First, the field is susceptible to stereotypes about engineers and computing professionals.

2. Second, the field is perceived as less open to women than it should be. The opportunity is there.

3. Third, many applications are used for undesirable goals, such as gathering excessive personal data or replacing jobs that don't need to be replaced.

Additional Comments:

I am poor at networking with other people and have always regretted it. Expanding your personal network is highly valuable.

TOM DROLET

PRINCIPAL ARCHITECT

JDA SOFTWARE GROUP

Prior Roles: Software Developer, Manager Software Development, Vice President, Group Vice President.

Education: BA Economics, Syracuse University; MBA, Finance, University of Hartford; MS, Computer Science, Johns Hopkins University.

"Play the long game."

How did you narrow down your interest(s) to your specific profession?

In graduate school, doing economics research as a graduate assistant, I found I enjoyed the computer aspects of the research most. I found a job after school, which combined the business and computer science fields, and was fortunate to have been able to stay and grow in the that field throughout my career (35+ years at this point).

When did you first realize that you were interested in your profession? If this occurred during high school, how did you pursue this interest as a high school student?

I had some interest in computers in high school (reading the now defunct *BYTE* and *Creative Computer Magazine*). I did not have access to an actual computer then (it was the '70s). I rekindled interest in graduate school while working with computers doing statistical research.

How did you break into the industry associated with your profession? What advice would you have for a high school student who is interested in breaking into the same industry?

It was difficult to find the first job in my field after graduating from school (graduate school).

Experience I had gained in school helped (work as graduate research assistant); it was essentially a numbers game of pursuing every job opportunity in the field I could find through ads, referrals, etc. (this was before the internet!).

Today, I would say you need to excel in school in math/computer science and gain any experience you can part time, through open source projects, etc. Always work to increase your knowledge and skills and keep up with the latest trends.

You may need to pick an area to specialize in—UX development, AI, cloud, DevOps, etc.

What are some aspects of your profession that the average high school student would not know but should know? What are some aspects that surprise you about your profession?

While programming skills are required, the need for "soft skills" is not always recognized. You will almost certainly be working on a team. Do you work well with others, and can you exchange ideas/viewpoints respectfully and clearly? Despite the reputation of software development as a "nerd" field, excellent communication skills and an ability to work well in a team is critical to succeeding!

Also, you should understand the business behind your work; usually, you are working on software for some particular business: retail, insurance, banking, etc. The more you understand that, the better you will be at your job.

If you were to hire the ideal job candidate for your profession, what kind of person would you be hiring? What qualities would this person have?

I'm looking for the following:

1. Success in prior work—that might be in school if the person is just entering the job market.
2. Communication skills.
3. Intelligence/curiosity—is the person interesting to talk to, well-rounded, curious about the world?
4. Specific skills in the area I'm recruiting for: for example, JavaScript development. (This is probably the least important because most candidates will likely have this; it's the other skills that will stand out.)
5. Enthusiasm!

Please provide a quote or mantra that you feel accurately reflects both you and your profession. It can be a quote generated by you or a quote from someone else. If the quote or mantra is from someone else, please specify who generated the quote or mantra.

"Play the long game." Don't know who originally said this. It means keeping long-term perspective and not getting caught up in minor irritations of the moment.

Please list your favorite three aspects of your profession.

1. Constant change—always new technologies/new approaches.
2. Ability to have impact by doing great work.
3. Working with some really smart people!

Please list your three least-favorite aspects about your profession.

1. Pressure of timelines leading to poor quality.
2. A tendency to follow hype/the latest shiny object.
3. Few people in my family understand what I do. :-)

VERTUME DUFAULT

SENIOR VICE PRESIDENT OF BUSINESS DEVELOPMENT

TRILLION TECHNOLOGY SOLUTIONS

Prior Roles: *Senior Director, Consulting Services—MarkLogic;*
Senior Director, Consulting Services—Oracle;
Technical Manager—Oracle;
Director, European Technical Services—InterCAP Graphics Systems;
Staff Developer—InterCAP Graphics Systems.

Education: *BS Computer Science—Virginia Tech; MBA—Virginia Tech.*

"In the land of the blind, the one-eyed man is king."

— Desiderius Erasmus

How did you narrow down your interest(s) to your specific profession?

Stumbled into it. Perhaps backed into it is a better explanation. After two years in college, I needed to claim a major and started by eliminating things I was not interested or skilled in and for which I had already taken classes that would count toward graduation. That left me with just a couple choices, and I selected CS [computer science], likely since I knew next to nothing about it: no (negative) preconceptions.

When did you first realize that you were interested in your profession? If this occurred during high school, how did you pursue this interest as a high school student?

I was better than many in problem-solving and had an ability to focus and persist, which enabled me to finish my programming assignments in school and the work I was assigned in my early career. My first few jobs were at great companies with great camaraderie, so I was having fun. So early success and enjoyment were the things that kept me going initially. However, within the first decade, I realized I was working with many folks who were heads and shoulders above me in both skills and interest, so I gradually moved to general business roles.

150

How did you break into the industry associated with your profession? What advice would you have for a high school student who is interested in breaking into the same industry?

I found a job that required specific skills and a specific degree (CS). Advice: get educated and experienced in your industry of interest.

What are some aspects of your profession that the average high school student would not know but should know? What are some aspects that surprise you about your profession?

Software development skills are table stakes for professional success, even though they are also the key to getting your first job. Get an education in everything you can. Learn how to work with others. Learn how to communicate effectively.

There is so much information and knowledge available to you; go get it and try to stay one page ahead of everyone else who is in the same arms race to acquire that knowledge.

Please list your favorite aspects of your profession.

Creative/maker-ish. Cosmopolitan. Challenging.

Please list your least-favorite aspects about your profession.

Sloppy (often), rapidly evolving.

Additional Comments:

Go get 'em.

CHRIS KRAFT

PROGRAM MANAGER

FEDERAL EMERGENCY MANAGEMENT AGENCY (FEMA)

Prior Roles: *Project Manager, Sr. Director/VP Systems.*

Education: *BS, Decision Sciences and Information Systems, George Mason University; JD, The George Washington University Law School.*

"We are all in this together; either we all succeed or we all fail."

How did you narrow down your interest(s) to your specific profession?

Over time, after overseeing many software projects and programs.

When did you first realize that you were interested in your profession? If this occurred during high school, how did you pursue this interest as a high school student?

After graduating from college, I worked for several accounting firms implementing enterprise resource planning (ERP) software applications.

These are large and complex software packages that businesses use to manage many back-office functions. Working with these software packages tapped into many of my interests and strengths, including technical skills, process improvement, interpersonal development and project management.

How did you break into the industry associated with your profession? What advice would you have for a high school student who is interested in breaking into the same industry?

I broke into the industry by deciding to leverage my information systems degree working for an accounting firm. I did not have the job offer I wanted when I graduated from college, so I pursued many accounting firms. I took a temporary position with a major accounting firm with the intention of finding a permanent job after the temporary assignment.

While working for the firm, I took on additional responsibilities building out a database to manage recruiting events, networked with other business groups, leveraged campus interview resources, and did everything possible to get hired.

I ended up receiving several offers from the accounting firm. Once hired into a consulting role, I continued to look for ways to align my interests and strengths to the opportunities available.

I encourage high school students to take on whatever opportunities exist within the areas they are interested in, including internships (paid/unpaid), co-ops, and part-time jobs. Get exposure to the areas you are interested in to see if they are a good fit. It is much easier to be successful when you tap into your strengths and interests.

What advice would you have for high school students who are interested in a profession that is similar to yours? Is there anything specific that you suggest that these high school students should do?

My recommendation to anyone interested in financial systems (or other ERP software applications) is to go deep into the technology and the functional business areas.

For example, with financial system implementations, it is very beneficial to have certified public accountants (CPAs) and others with business knowledge to define system requirements. It is also beneficial to have team members who understand the technology.

I believe the best resources can draw from both the business and technical knowledge.

What are some aspects of your profession that the average high school student would not know but should know? What are some aspects that surprise you about your profession?

Leadership, organizational change management, large-scale project management, and operational organizational realities.

Some of these take time to learn and others can be taught in school. It surprises me how easy it is to fail, or not maximize your potential, by thinking you understand more than you do. Take time to learn from people who have experience, work hard/smart, and try to find work-life balance.

If you were to hire the ideal job candidate for your profession, what kind of person would you be hiring? What qualities would this person have?

The ideal candidate would be someone who is smart, has a well-rounded education, understands the broad functional areas (financial management), and has experience working on software implementations. It is important to be detail-oriented, independent, and able to work effectively on a team.

Please list your favorite three aspects of your profession.

1. Dynamic—many unforeseen challenges that keep the work interesting.
2. Leadership—the opportunity to lead people and projects.
3. Change—the ability to implement real, tangible changes that make organizations more efficient and more capable of performing their mission.

Please list your three least-favorite aspects about your profession.

1. Documentation—sometimes there's too much.

2. Conflict—there can be lots of conflict when trying to keep a project on schedule and making sure everyone delivers.

3. Meetings—too many meetings make it hard to get actual work done.

ALAN NASH

PRESIDENT AND SOLE PROPRIETOR

RADIUS DEVELOPMENT
[ADVANCED ANALYTICS, MACHINE LEARNING, & SIGNAL PROCESSING]

Prior Roles: Senior Engineer, Aegis Engineering, 1989–1994; Vice President, Practical Imagineering, Inc. 1994–2004; Director, Signals Intelligence Systems, BAE Systems, 2004–2009.

Education: BS EE, MIT, 1989; Some graduate work, George Mason University, 1992–1994.

"If I wasn't getting paid, I'd probably be doing something similar to this anyway."

How did you narrow down your interest(s) to your specific profession?

As a college junior, I met some of my older sister's friends who worked in my field. They brought me in for a quick interview over a weekend that resulted in a summer job offer. I was impressed that they came in just to meet me, so I took it and eventually got a full-time job with them after graduating. So, I just kind of fell into it.

When did you first realize that you were interested in your profession? If this occurred during high school, how did you pursue this interest as a high school student?

I was always interested in technology, math, computers, and electronics. I enjoyed physics, chemistry, and math the most in high school. When it came time for college, I talked to my dad, and he suggested electrical engineering, which seemed like a good fit. I didn't feel like I had the intuition for mechanical systems as much as logical ones, so I went for EE [electrical engineering].

How did you break into the industry associated with your profession? What advice would you have for a high school student who is interested in breaking into the same industry?

Technology work is in demand, so the key thing is to get experience with programming and to pair that with another interest area, whether it's network security, biomedical applications, artificial intelligence, robotics, data storage, user interface design, laboratory research, farming, or whatever.

The power of software and technology will affect every conceivable field and organization, and all companies will need technology workers to survive and prosper.

What advice would you have for high school students who are interested in a profession that is similar to yours? Is there anything specific that you suggest that these high school students should do?

One thing that would have really helped me would have been to get into some offices or work spaces where actual work gets done. Seeing what it's like in a lab, cubicle office, formal office, or field site can give a good idea what it would be like to spend time there. What's on TV and the movies isn't usually an accurate representation, but some of them are not far off in some ways.

What are some aspects of your profession that the average high school student would not know but should know? What are some aspects that surprise you about your profession?

I think it is hard to realize how much time and energy is spent on the process of doing engineering work, rather than the work itself. What I mean is that there are so many jobs involved with developing a technology product or service that it's hard to imagine. Most people, as I did, probably envision hacking away at code most of the time, but there is a lot of planning, coordination, training, compliance testing, revision control, presentations, cost estimating, time estimating, reviews, proposals, and so forth that not only require time and effort but also teamwork and communication between team members.

If you were to hire the ideal job candidate for your profession, what kind of person would you be hiring? What qualities would this person have?

Someone who enjoys working with data in various forms, who can quickly learn and use programming tools and languages, and who likes the feeling of creating things. Being interested is the most important; if you are motivated and like what you are doing, you will probably do it well and keep improving.

Please provide a quote or mantra that you feel accurately reflects both you and your profession. It can be a quote generated by you or a quote from someone else. If the quote or mantra is from someone else, please specify who generated the quote or mantra.

"If I wasn't getting paid, I'd probably be doing something similar to this anyway." Various coworkers and I came up with this idea early on in my career since I tend to fiddle around with similar things at home as at work; sometimes I think it is accurate.

What are your favorite and least-favorite parts about your profession?

I think my favorite part is when I can combine mathematical concepts with software to come up with ways of interpreting or displaying data that yield answers. It's a lot like solving a puzzle to me, and it's gratifying to see answers flow out of something I created.

My least-favorite part is doing proposals and bids—at least the ones that don't end up winning jobs!

MATT PROBUS

CHIEF EXECUTIVE OFFICER

SKOOLAR
[WEB APP FOR COLLEGE STUDENTS]

Prior Roles: *Vice President of Engineering, Chief Information Officer, Chief Technology Officer, General Manager, President.*

Education: *BS Computer Science, Virginia Tech.*

"Genius is one percent inspiration, ninety-nine percent perspiration."

— *Thomas Edison*

How did you narrow down your interest(s) to your specific profession?

By taking related classes and career-interest tests and talking with people in various professions.

When did you first realize that you were interested in your profession? If this occurred during high school, how did you pursue this interest as a high school student?

In high school, I took the few computer science classes available at the time and enjoyed them. I also participated in an Explorer post (affiliated with Boy Scouts) focused on software, during high school.

How did you break into the industry associated with your profession? What advice would you have for a high school student who is interested in breaking into the same industry?

I got a summer internship with Computer Sciences Corp. after my first year of college, which was both insightful and good for my resume. During college, I took courses in artificial intelligence, which the hiring manager for my first career position cited as key in attracting his attention.

Earning a degree in computer science from a reputable university, along with a good GPA, is nearly guaranteed to attract employers.

What advice would you have for high school students who are interested in a profession that is similar to yours? Is there anything specific that you suggest that these high school students should do?

For high school students, I would recommend, if they haven't done so already, building their own computer, learning a programming language, and getting involved in related extracurricular activities, such as hackathons and/or writing their own apps.

What are some aspects of your profession that the average high school student would not know but should know? What are some aspects that surprise you about your profession?

Courses in writing, public speaking, management, and accounting are all very important to anyone interested in moving up or running a technology department or company, just like in any other profession.

What surprises me about my profession is how quickly technical skills can become out of date if someone isn't regularly learning the latest tools.

If you were to hire the ideal job candidate for your profession, what kind of person would you be hiring? What qualities would this person have?

I'd hire someone who has a passionate interest in our work. Someone who didn't get into the field just to get a job but instead because he/she/they loves working in this field. The person would be driven to learn everything possible to succeed and would want to be an expert in our industry. The person would also be a team player who can work productively with others.

Please provide a quote or mantra that you feel accurately reflects both you and your profession. It can be a quote generated by you or a quote from someone else. If the quote or mantra is from someone else, please specify who generated the quote or mantra.

"Genius is one percent inspiration, ninety-nine percent perspiration." — Thomas Edison

Whatever I have ever accomplished is more attributed to hard work than to raw intelligence.

Please list your favorite three aspects of your profession.

1. With very few people and limited resources, we can create something of benefit to millions, if not billions, of people.

2. The benefits of our work can be very tangible in terms of savings of time, money, and effort.

3. The industry is wide open; compared to many professions, your ability is more important than your pedigree.

Please list your three least-favorite aspects about your profession.

1. What you spent countless hours learning a few years ago is not necessarily relevant any more.

2. Marketing hype often exaggerates or distorts the reality.

3. Too many people are willing to exploit technology for unethical purposes.

Additional Comments:

It's hard for me to imagine any field being more exciting for a high school student to follow than technology.

LARRY ROSHFELD

CHIEF EXECUTIVE OFFICER

AFFIRMLOGIC [COMPUTER SOFTWARE]

Education: BA Clark University; MA Harvard University.

"The only thing standing between you and your goals is the bullshit story you keep telling yourself as to why you can't achieve it."

— Author unknown

How did you narrow down your interest(s) to your specific profession?

I fell into it accidentally. I finished my master's and wasn't sure if I wanted to spend the time to get my PhD, so I traveled for a while, and then just took a job to pay the bills. I ended up loving the field and sticking with it.

When did you first realize that you were interested in your profession? If this occurred during high school, how did you pursue this interest as a high school student?

When I was twenty-five years old.

How did you break into the industry associated with your profession? What advice would you have for a high school student who is interested in breaking into the same industry?

I'd actually recommend that high school students not worry about professions and focus on studying the subjects they enjoy (when they have options). There are so many fields of which typical high school students are unaware; I think focusing too early is a bad idea.

160

What advice would you have for high school students who are interested in a profession that is similar to yours? Is there anything specific that you suggest that these high school students should do?

The key to executive management is to become an "expert generalist," so you have deep expertise in one area (e.g., engineering, marketing, sales, etc.) and strong familiarity with others.

What are some aspects of your profession that the average high school student would not know but should know? What are some aspects that surprise you about your profession?

Leadership, management, strategy, finance.

Please list your favorite three aspects of your profession.

Creativity, collaboration, vision.

Please list your three least-favorite aspects about your profession.

Personnel management, accounting, hiring.

EDWARD SALWIN

SOFTWARE DEVELOPER

INTRAFI NETWORK

Prior Roles: *I've worked as a software developer my whole career, although I dabbled with business development during my first two years after college.*

Education: *BS Information Systems from Carnegie Mellon University; MS Information Technology—eBusiness from Carnegie Mellon University.*

"Perfection is achieved not when there is nothing more to add but rather when there is nothing more to take away."

— *Antoine de Saint*

How did you narrow down your interest(s) to your specific profession?

I sought a balance between what I like (and dislike), what I'm good at, and what's marketable.

When did you first realize that you were interested in your profession? If this occurred during high school, how did you pursue this interest as a high school student?

I began programming computers in elementary school, but didn't consider it for my profession until my senior year of college.

In high school, I programmed applications for fun and for classes. If you're already performing a skill for fun, definitely pay attention to that.

How did you break into the industry associated with your profession? What advice would you have for a high school student who is interested in breaking into the same industry?

During my senior year of high school, my dad set me up with a website design internship through an

162

acquaintance. Is that cheating? Try to exercise your skills in extracurricular activities or internships.

What advice would you have for high school students who are interested in a profession that is similar to yours? Is there anything specific that you suggest that these high school students should do?

Program computers on your own or as part of a club or open source project.

What are some aspects of your profession that the average high school student would not know but should know? What are some aspects that surprise you about your profession?

Developing software for a personal project is very different from developing software for an organization. The social aspects (of working with other people and integrating your software with that of other developers) adds many layers of complexity.

If you were to hire the ideal job candidate for your profession, what kind of person would you be hiring? What qualities would this person have?

Candidates should care about their work and have a decent temperament.

Please list your favorite three aspects of your profession.

1. I can specialize in certain areas while still exploring new challenges and technologies.
2. I don't need to work too, too much with other people (compared to business people).
3. Tech culture.

Please list your three least-favorite aspects about your profession.

1. Sometimes, I spend "too" much time on a computer.
2. Negotiating with stakeholders (e.g., explaining how long something will take, what you can and can't deliver, etc.).
3. Sometimes, the technologies and challenges change "too" quickly.

How has your industry changed since the pandemic?

As a software developer, I am very fortunate and grateful to work in an industry that held up relatively well during the pandemic since we perform much of our work with just a computer. Like many jobs, we suffered a loss of communication bandwidth as we cannot meet in person now, but we have not suffered nearly as much as so many other positions.

JAMES SHANNON

TECHNOLOGY GENERAL MANAGER

CONDUENT

Prior Roles: Software Developer, Systems Engineer, Product Manager, Software Development Manager.

Education: BS, History and Political Science, Frostburg State University; BS, Mathematics, University of Maryland; MS, Computer Science, Johns Hopkins University.

> *"A scout is trustworthy, loyal, helpful, friendly, courteous, kind, obedient, cheerful, thrifty, brave, and reverent."*

How did you narrow down your interest(s) to your specific profession?

I initially wanted to join the Foreign Service. However, there were a few obstacles standing in my way (experience, competition), so that dream sort of died. While trying to do that, I continued to work on my math degree thinking that being a math teacher would be a good idea. I had always liked teaching and working with others. So, I did take some computer science classes while working on my math. I fell in love with computer science and computer programming, and it just sort of all fell into place. I loved creating, and it was a good way to spend my hours working. After that, things just went the way they did. So now I manage (teach) and mentor my team as we deliver systems to our clients.

When did you first realize that you were interested in your profession? If this occurred during high school, how did you pursue this interest as a high school student?

Post college. I really had no idea what I wanted to do during high school.

How did you break into the industry associated with your profession? What advice would you have for a high school student who is interested in breaking into the same industry?

After college, I had really no coaching on finding a job, so I found a job via the *Washington Post* Help Wanted ads. That was for my first job, and my second job as well. After that, it was more from other colleagues or headhunters.

For my son, he did internships during college. That really helped him, and he set up good contacts as he went forward.

So, at this point, I suggest attempting to get an internship or a summer job opportunity at a technology-type firm.

What advice would you have for high school students who are interested in a profession that is similar to yours? Is there anything specific that you suggest that these high school students should do?

You need to be willing to keep learning. In the technical area, everything is always changing, and you need to be a person who loves to learn and to keep up with new ideas and technologies.

Pursue what you like to do.

Quite honestly, learning technical skills, no matter your overall career interests, will be key. I have so much fun just helping people learn how to use their iPhones or Excel spreadsheets.

If you are interested in technology, it is important to have a strong mathematical/logical thinking background. A lot of musicians are great computer wizards.

I suggest that you really spend time learning how to communicate and how to write. Being able to communicate effectively is a key skill set.

What are some aspects of your profession that the average high school student would not know but should know? What are some aspects that surprise you about your profession?

We get involved with many, many different situations that are very rewarding. You can compare it to other very creative professions: musician, artist, architect, builder. If you enjoy the start of a new project, working on a project, and then the overall completion of a project, then this is a good profession.

There are many opportunities to meet and discuss real-world issues, and potential solutions to these problems as we (the larger WE) look to automation and other tools to allow our world to work more efficiently. It can be very rewarding personally to realize that the work you do actually helps the environment, or helps save lives.

If you were to hire the ideal job candidate for your profession, what kind of person would you be hiring? What qualities would this person have?

1. Good communications skills.
2. A can-do attitude.
3. The ability to learn new skills.
4. Desire to tackle new issues or tackle new problems.
5. Flexibility in assignments. Some assignments are fun. Others are not but need to be done.

Please provide a quote or mantra that you feel accurately reflects both you and your profession. It can be a quote generated by you or a quote from someone else. If the quote or mantra is from someone else, please specify who generated the quote or mantra.

I was a Boy Scout, and I try to practice the scout law:

"A scout is trustworthy, loyal, helpful, friendly, courteous, kind, obedient, cheerful, thrifty, brave, and reverent."

Try to apply that to your daily life in how you treat people. It will go a long way.

Please list your favorite three aspects of your profession.

1. Meeting people from all over the world.
2. Delivering solutions to our clients that solve real-world problems.
3. Travel.

Please list your three least-favorite aspects about your profession.

1. Sometimes the need to make profits drives poor short-term decisions.
2. Unfortunately, sometimes you work a lot. :)
3. If a project goes badly, tough discussions can occur.

CONNIE TAYLOR

VICE PRESIDENT OF SOFTWARE DEVELOPMENT

MANHATTAN ASSOCIATES

Prior Roles: *Software Developer, Quality Manager, Project Director, Consultant.*

Education: *BS Mathematical Science—University of North Carolina at Chapel Hill; MS Computer Science—Johns Hopkins University.*

"Prolific developers don't always write a lot of code; instead they solve a lot of problems. The two things are not the same."

— J. Chambers

How did you narrow down your interest(s) to your specific profession?

I liked solving problems and math from an early age. I discovered programming in college and thought it was very interesting and a fun way to use my problem-solving skills.

When did you first realize that you were interested in your profession? If this occurred during high school, how did you pursue this interest as a high school student?

I really did not know much about software development until college and my first job. I liked math in high school, so I pursued that as my major.

How did you break into the industry associated with your profession? What advice would you have for a high school student who is interested in breaking into the same industry?

I started in a consulting company (Booz Allen Hamilton), which was a great way to get a broad perspective on business, customer interaction, and problem-solving experience in business. I also did an internship in college.

What advice would you have for high school students who are interested in a profession that is similar to yours? Is there anything specific that you suggest that these high school students should do?

I would recommend that you pick a math or science college degree to break into this industry. If you are really sharp, it is possible to get certificates and not a college degree, but I think it is harder to land the first job and will limit your earning potential.

What are some aspects of your profession that the average high school student would not know but should know? What are some aspects that surprise you about your profession?

There are many different facets of software development that are not just being a geek and programming. You can be a business analyst and develop requirements for software developers; you can be a tester; or you can be a front-end designer. I was surprised at how creative software development was until I became more involved.

If you were to hire the ideal job candidate for your profession, what kind of person would you be hiring? What qualities would this person have?

Great problem-solver, able to learn new things quickly, team player, strong communicator.

Please list your favorite three aspects of your profession.

1. Creative and smart people you work with.
2. You can work in a lot of different industries if you are in software development.
3. Overall, the pay is good in this field.

Please list your three least-favorite aspects about your profession.

1. Software is always changing; it is VERY hard to commit to dates.
2. Too much outsourcing to other countries; focus more on cost than quality.
3. As a manager, it is very hard to find candidates to fill positions. We need more people choosing this field in the US!

ALISON GRIZZLE

DIRECTOR OF ORGANIZATIONAL DEVELOPMENT

STARNES MEDIA

Prior Roles: *Mathematics Teacher—fourteen years; Teacher Mentor—one year; Administrator at State Department of Education—three years.*

Education: *BA, Double Major Mathematics and English Literature—Denison University; MA, Secondary Education with Mathematics focus—University of Alabama at Birmingham; EdD, Teacher Leadership—Walden University; MEd Instructional Leadership— University of Montevallo; Certified Graduate of Coach University.*

"The growth and development of people is the highest calling of leadership."

— *Harvey Firestone*

"Without continual growth and progress, such words as improvement, achievement, and success have no meaning."

— *Benjamin Franklin*

How did you narrow down your interest(s) to your specific profession?

Passions evolve. Skills sharpen. Life changes. Each job, each choice, each company has a season. Sometimes those seasons are long and sometimes the seasons are short. And transitions between roles, between employers, and between industries are rewarding, yet challenging.

I began by following a passion to teach. I wanted to teach because I had a talent for presentation, a talent for breaking down complicated concepts into manageable pieces of information. I knew that I could teach, but I wanted to maximize impact, so I followed my heart to a community that did not have a reputation for always being able to secure top talent. I went to a community where many referred to students as "at risk" and referred to the community as "underserved." I narrowed to this beginning because my father encouraged me to follow my heart. He encouraged me to choose a job in which I felt as if I got "paid to play."

In those fifteen years, I learned more about myself, my perceptions, my deficit-filled language, social justice, issues of race and class, etc., more than I could ever describe. The students were bubbling with potential but lacking access to power structures, struggling to knock down multiple barriers but lacking all the resources needed to do so, filled with energy but lacking opportunities, and overflowing with ideas but lacking mentors. The students were always climbing uphill. The days were long. Each day, I returned home emotionally and physically exhausted. It was extremely rewarding but extremely difficult.

After leaving the classroom, I moved into more of a consulting and strategy role with the State Department of Education. I worked with multiple school districts throughout the state assessing the components of effective teaching and how that impacts teacher evaluation and professional learning.

My skills of mentoring, creating professional learning, coaching, evaluation systems, and strategic planning that I gained during my years on leadership teams as a teacher and leading a team at the State Department prepared me for my current role in organizational development.

When did you first realize that you were interested in your profession? If this occurred during high school, how did you pursue this interest as a high school student?

I fought the idea of becoming a teacher because I was scared of the pay. I followed my "calling," which I finally accepted and understood shortly after graduating from college. I learned that the description of the career as a "calling" often limits people's perception of the complexity of this particular career choice. Teaching is highly technical and requires the mastery of a very complex set of skills. The professional expertise to be a great teacher is very high. One of the challenges in this career is that everybody attended school from K–12, so everybody thinks that they know how to accomplish the daily tasks of a teacher. From politicians to parents, outside stakeholders believe that they understand the problems greater than the people who are doing the work.

During my fifteenth year, I was named Alabama Teacher of the Year. This honor put me at the table with many policy makers, and I found a true love for policy and strategy, specifically around teacher quality and school quality. This put me on a new path in education.

And, eventually, I used these skills to join my entrepreneur husband in the business that I had helped to build for nine years. In 2009, when I began dating Dan, he was the only full-time employee of Starnes Media. He had one local community newspaper that was direct-mailed to 12,000 homes. Over the next nine years, he and I worked as a team to grow the reach of community journalism, as well as the revenue of the company. At the time that I entered the business fulltime in 2017, we had grown to seven local community papers direct-mailed to nearly 120,000 homes and a full-service digital marketing agency. I came into the company to help create clear performance objectives and coach the staff of thirty on reaching clearly defined measures. This also entailed working with people to clearly document organizational processes that were fundamental to the company's success.

What advice would you have for a high school student who is interested in breaking into the same industry?

Teaching—Secure necessary credentials.

Advice—Make sure that you have a passion for content and a passion for developing students and helping children to meet individualized goals.

Education leadership—Experience success in the classroom; secure credentials.

Advice—Teach first. Understand the nuances of the profession. Create a portfolio of documented successes.

Organizational development—Gain experience in strategic planning, creation of individualized performance goals, development of objective-based evaluation systems, and certification in coaching.

Advice—Learn to listen, learn to coach, and be a constant student of human interactions and management.

What advice would you have for high school students who are interested in a profession that is similar to yours? Is there anything specific that you suggest that these high school students should do?

Regardless of what you perceive to be your interest or your passion, spend a week in someone else's shoes. Find someone to shadow. Make sure that you have experienced the career prior to investing and going "all in."

Internships are great, but, you need to shadow the person in the actual job for a week. In an internship, you will be given tasks that are helpful to the company that don't necessarily give you an idea of the career. Follow a person's schedule, shadow a person, and engage in the day-to-day tasks. Make sure you would enjoy the position.

What are some aspects of your profession that the average high school student would not know but should know? What are some aspects that surprise you about your profession?

Teaching—

1. It is much more complicated than it looks.
2. Students are unpredictable in ways that are good and bad.
3. Top-down decisions create barriers that you aren't expecting.
4. Everyone thinks that he/she/they could do the job.
5. Hours are long.
6. Paperwork and documentation can be brutal.
7. The rewards last for years.
8. If you are good, students will still contact you fifteen years later to tell you that you are loved.

Education administration—

1. Politicians impact policy.
2. People far removed from the classroom make decisions that impact the teacher.
3. Change is extremely slow.
4. Bureaucracy at the state level is absurd.

Organizational development—

1. Not everyone embraces change.
2. Coaching people through change is challenging but rewarding.
3. Managing people can be complex.
4. If you own a business, know that many have an 8 a.m.–5 p.m. mentality; goal-based management is difficult when people want to punch a clock.
5. It is critical to determine how to align individual goals with company goals to make

sure that everyone is pushing to the same finish line.

If you were to hire the ideal job candidate for your profession, what kind of person would you be hiring? What qualities would this person have?

- Strategic, critical thinker
- Listener
- Clear communicator
- Good writer
- Lifelong learner
- Reader of people and situations
- High in cognitive processing and emotional intelligence

Please list your favorite aspects of your profession.

1. Teaching—Watching students succeed.
2. Education leadership—Watching teachers modify their practices to better impact students.
3. Organizational development—Helping people meet their goals through coaching and process creation.

Please list your least-favorite aspects about your profession.

1. Teaching—Paperwork, obstinate students.
2. Education leadership—Bureaucratic structures.
3. Organizational development—Working with people who don't see issues with "the way things are"… when people don't want to get "unstuck."

BARB REHM

FORMER EDITOR-IN-CHIEF

AMERICAN BANKER

Prior Roles: Reporter, Natural Gas Week, a weekly newsletter covering the natural gas industry; Reporter, Energy Week, a weekly newsletter covering the energy industry; Joined American Banker in 1987 as a Reporter and was promoted to Deputy Washington Bureau Chief, Washington Bureau Chief, Senior Editor, and Managing Editor over twenty years before becoming Editor-in-Chief.

Education: BA U. of Missouri-Columbia, Speech; MA U. of Missouri-Columbia, Journalism.

"If your mother tells you she loves you, check it out."

"Make one more call."

How did you narrow down your interest(s) to your specific profession?

I participated extensively in student government during my undergraduate years and decided I should go to grad school, and University of Missouri has an excellent journalism school. So I applied, got in, and fell in love with reporting and writing the news.

When did you first realize that you were interested in your profession? If this occurred during high school, how did you pursue this interest as a high school student?

Toward the end of my undergraduate degree—so no, I did not give much thought to a career in high school.

How did you break into the industry associated with your profession? What advice would you have for a high school student who is interested in breaking into the same industry?

I spent my last semester of grad school in Washington, DC, working in the university's news bureau. That helped me "break in" because it gave me concrete evidence—actual stories in real newspapers—to offer potential employers. If a student's high school has a newspaper, that would be a great start. If it doesn't, the yearbook would be a decent substitute. Anything that exposes you to writing, editing, layout, and design would be helpful.

What advice would you have for high school students who are interested in a profession that is similar to yours? Is there anything specific that you suggest that these high school students should do?

Perhaps an additional idea would be to intern or even volunteer at a local newspaper.

What are some aspects of your profession that the average high school student would not know but should know? What are some aspects that surprise you about your profession?

Many different types of people make successful journalists. When I started, I thought only outgoing types could succeed, but over the years I have realized that many of the best reporters are quite introverted. They listen well and draw sources out with silence. Gaps in conversation make many people uncomfortable, so they fill the void and say more than they might with a more extroverted reporter.

If you were to hire the ideal job candidate for your profession, what kind of person would you be hiring? What qualities would this person have?

Curiosity is key, especially for reporters. You have to want to ask people questions. The ability to synthesize a lot of (often conflicting) information is important, too.

Please provide a quote or mantra that you feel accurately reflects both you and your profession. It can be a quote generated by you or a quote from someone else.

Every journalist has heard this one: "If your mother tells you she loves you, check it out." It underscores the importance of ensuring you get your facts right.

I think my personal mantra was: "Make one more call." Every time I did, I learned something necessary.

Please list your favorite three aspects of your profession.

1. Variety—Every day was different.
2. Autonomy—Journalists are in charge of their beats/stories, so they have a lot of independence.
3. Satisfaction—Every day the paper came out, and it was a satisfying way to end the day (this is less true today, as the internet has made the news cycle 24/7).

Please list your three least-favorite aspects about your profession.

1. Deadlines—You often have to file your stories before you feel they are finished to make deadline.
2. Space—Again this isn't true today, but before the rise of online news, I used to hate watching my stories get cut to fit the space on the page.
3. Pay—Friends who went into PR [public relations] made a lot more money than I did.

Additional Comments:

Technology has clearly changed journalism, but, at its heart, it is still about gathering and disseminating information to inform an audience. That's a big responsibility and, most days, a lot of fun.

14 NONPROFIT ADMINISTRATION

Betsy Bates
EXECUTIVE DIRECTOR
Children's Chorus of Washington 179

BETSY BATES

EXECUTIVE DIRECTOR

CHILDREN'S CHORUS OF WASHINGTON

Prior Roles: Consultant, Operations Manager, and Co-Owner of a small marketing company, Freelance Singer.

Education: BA in Music, St. Mary's College of Maryland; Graduate Performance Diploma in Voice, The Peabody Institute of Johns Hopkins University.

How did you narrow down your interest(s) to your specific profession?

I'd been singing since childhood, but I also had strong computer and math skills. I kept singing, and I learned to code. Through a business I ran with my husband, I learned about budgeting, project management, and marketing. I just kept doing interesting projects, and this job aligns many of my interests in one position.

When did you first realize that you were interested in your profession? If this occurred during high school, how did you pursue this interest as a high school student?

I did things I liked, and I did them a lot. I sang in chorus and madrigals, did plays and musicals, and played piano. I also excelled at science, math, and writing. I didn't know I would be an executive director one day. I studied hard and tried new things.

How did you break into the industry associated with your profession? What advice would you have for a high school student who is interested in breaking into the same industry?

It was through good timing and the relationships I had built. I also stand by my work, and I'm passionate about doing things right and well.

When you care about doing a good job, and do good work, people want to work with you, and they want to tell their friends and colleagues about you, too.

What advice would you have for high school students who are interested in a profession that is similar to yours? Is there anything specific that you suggest that these high school students should do?

Your first job will probably not be fun. Your first five jobs might not be fun. But you will learn something valuable from every job you do.

Keep looking for interesting people and projects that excite you. Do a small part for something big that you really care about, and then do a little more the next time. Don't try to do all the things.

Pick one or two things that you can do really well, and focus your time and energy. It's great to be well-rounded, but you can't have a dozen hobbies if you want to be great at something.

What are some aspects of your profession that the average high school student would not know but should know? What are some aspects that surprise you about your profession?

So much of my success depends on other people. When you are the boss, you need a really strong team around you, and you don't build that overnight. I can only be great at my job if my staff members are able to do their jobs well. Every person on a team is important. Find how you can be the best asset to your team, and go hard in that direction.

Everyone does grunt work sometimes, but you should also find spaces where you can really shine, no matter your role.

Being the boss can also be very lonely. You are responsible for a lot of people and money or other resources. It's a lot of stress sometimes. It can be very rewarding, but you often have one good thing that happens and that other people know about, and you only hear about the ten bad things

or problems that need fixing. You have to pace yourself, and accept that there will be things left undone. There is no perfect day in this job.

If you were to hire the ideal job candidate for your profession, what kind of person would you be hiring? What qualities would this person have?

Curious; kind; brave; has strong opinions but is able to listen to other perspectives; able to wade through red tape; finds purpose in the work; invested in collaborating.

Please provide a quote or mantra that you feel accurately reflects both you and your profession. It can be a quote generated by you or a quote from someone else. If the quote or mantra is from someone else, please specify who generated the quote or mantra.

Keep calm and carry on, maybe. Or, start with great art, as Michael Kaiser of the DeVos Institute of Arts Management would say. Just do it. Don't stop. I'm not much into mantras, but now I can't help myself.

Please list your favorite three aspects of your profession.

1. I love making an event run smoothly. It's not just about what's presented on stage; the rest of the experience matters, too.

2. Staying intimately connected to music-making, but not having to be the performer. This is rewarding, exciting, and many days a huge relief.

3. Surprisingly, since I am an introvert, I love the chance to work with so many people. I have stimulating conversations with parents, students, staff, board members, colleagues, organizations, and music lovers. I love to talk about how we can make the program better,

how we can create new projects together, or how the chorus has impacted a child's life.

Please list your three least-favorite aspects about your profession.

1. Dealing with government agencies to keep our various registrations current. It's time-consuming and happens annually.
2. Being constrained by funding.
3. People's misconceptions about how nonprofits should be run, funded, staffed, etc.

How has your industry changed since the pandemic?

Responding to the pandemic and planning for its longer-term impacts has required a lot of patience, perseverance, creativity, and solution-oriented thinking. This experience has increased the sense of uncertainty but also underscores the importance of nonprofit work. We are concerned about future enrollment and philanthropic giving, but we are encouraged by positive feedback from our community and high participation rates from our students during this stay-at-home period. This time is also an opportunity to challenge the way things have been, because, in a situation where we can't gather in person, we have to innovate because the arts are more important than ever. We are focusing on doing what we can do rather than all of the things we used to be able to do. This is the approach that has allowed us to continue progressing, and it's what will serve our mission until we can safely be together again in person.

15 PSYCHOLOGY

MAUREEN MANNING

SCHOOL PSYCHOLOGIST

GREEN TREE SCHOOL & SERVICES

Prior Roles: *Contracted School Psychologist, Anne Arundel County Public Schools (AACPS), Annapolis, MD; School Psychologist, Anne Arundel County Public Schools (AACPS), Annapolis, MD; School Psychology Intern, New Orleans Public Schools, New Orleans, LA; Assistant Professor, Department of Psychology, Towson University, Towson, MD; Adjunct Faculty, Department of Psychology, Towson University, Towson, MD; Instructor, School of Education, University of Delaware, Newark, DE; Research Assistant, School of Education, University of Delaware, Newark, DE; Tutor, Christina School District, Newark, DE; Extended Daily Substitute, Chester County Intermediate Unit, Exton, PA; Therapeutic Staff Support, United Staffing Services, Philadelphia, PA; Therapeutic Activity Aide, Lancaster Family Resource Center, Lancaster, PA; Intern, The Help Counseling Center, West Chester, PA; Camp Counselor, West Chester Recreation, West Chester, PA.*

Education: *PhD of Philosophy in Education, University of Delaware, Newark, DE; MA in School Psychology, University of Delaware, Newark, DE; BS in Education and BS in Psychology, St. Joseph's University, Philadelphia, PA.*

"School psychologists are change agents."

How did you narrow down your interest(s) to your specific profession?

I knew I was interested in something related to education and psychology, so I majored in both during college. I did not discover the career of school psychology until college.

During college, a friend told me that I must want to be a school psychologist (like her mom) because of my double major. I had never heard of school psychology before, but, after looking further into it, it seemed like it was exactly what I had been searching for—the perfect blend of my interests and skills.

How did you break into the industry associated with your profession? What advice would you have for a high school student who is interested in breaking into the same industry?

Becoming a school psychologist requires at least two years of graduate school study followed by a year-long internship. I elected to pursue my PhD, so I did several extra years of coursework before my internship. During this time, I completed four practicum experiences in local schools before completing my internship in New Orleans public schools. I was well-prepared for securing a job as a school psychologist based on my graduate training, practicum experiences, and internship.

As a high school student, I frequently worked with children, including by babysitting, tutoring, and working as a summer camp counselor. While in college, I gained experience working with children with developmental delays and mental health difficulties, such as working as a therapeutic staff support (TSS) at summer camp and in students' homes.

I would advise high school students to try to do the same, gaining experience with children who develop typically and those who develop atypically.

Many opportunities exist for high school students to volunteer with organizations, like Best Buddies or Special Olympics, or to tutor students at local schools.

In addition, high school students should take advantage of opportunities to demonstrate leadership within their current environment, as there are likely many opportunities to bring about change.

If there is a problem, how can you help solve it? For example, how can you reduce bullying at your school? How can you help reduce the stigma of mental illness? How can you help increase students' rates of seeking help for academic, social, or emotional concerns? How can you improve the climate of your school?

What advice would you have for high school students who are interested in a profession that is similar to yours? Is there anything specific that you suggest that these high school students should do?

I would advise high school students to shadow a few school psychologists in a few different areas (e.g., school districts, states) to help determine if this a career they would like to pursue.

The job varies quite a bit depending on where school psychologists are employed, where the school psychologists are trained, and how proactive school psychologists are in seeking

responsibilities that may be viewed as outside their job role.

I would also advise students to check out the website of the National Association of School Psychologists (NASP) at www.nasponline.org. This website has a great deal of information about the role of school psychologists and the many ways in which school psychologists assist students, teachers, parents, and school communities. In particular, I would advise checking out the NASP practice model, which highlights the ten domains of school psychology practice. The NASP website can also connect high school students with their state school psychology associations and help them find a mentor in the field.

What are some aspects of your profession that the average high school student would not know but should know? What are some aspects that surprise you about your profession?

The average high school student may not know this career exists or may not know the many different opportunities available to a school psychologist.

According to US News & World Report, school psychology is ranked as the no. 2 best social service job and has consistently ranked among the top two social service professions for the past three years. The Bureau of Labor Statistics predicts a fourteen percent increase in the profession as awareness of the need for school-based mental health services grows.

If you were to hire the ideal job candidate for your profession, what kind of person would you be hiring? What qualities would this person have?

When I make hiring decisions, I look for individuals who have excellent problem-solving skills, who take initiative, and who seek to improve systems and bring about positive changes for students, staff, and school communities.

Please provide a quote or mantra that you feel accurately reflects both you and your profession. It can be a quote generated by you or a quote from someone else. If the quote or mantra is from someone else, please specify who generated the quote or mantra.

"School psychologists are change agents."

I can't take credit for this quote, nor can I attribute it to one person in particular. This is a common mantra in the field. For example, the philosophy was built into the graduate program I attended at the University of Delaware, as well as the graduate program in which I taught at Towson University.

Please list your favorite three aspects of your profession.

1. The opportunity to change students' lives for the better.
2. The opportunity to improve school systems.
3. The opportunity to do something different every day.

Please list your three least-favorite aspects about your profession.

1. The stress level can be very high.
2. It can be difficult to maintain work-life balance.
3. The role is often misunderstood.

Key Takeaways...

I want to share some key takeaways from the professionals featured in the book.

1. **You don't already know what you want to do? That's fine.** Professionals consistently reiterated that it is perfectly fine to not know what you want to do during your high school and early college years. The majority of respondents identified their career interests during or after college, and all are plenty successful in their current careers.

2. **Sometimes, it does not matter what position you get; the important part is breaking into the industry, not the stature of the work or position.** Be proactive in pursuing opportunities; in general, they are not going to just appear out of nowhere, and you can create your own luck.

3. **Luck appreciates preparation.** When you want to get lucky and break into an industry, be as prepared as you can possibly be. Know the jargon associated with that industry, cultivate your leadership and communication skills, and prepare yourself as well as you can so that you are ready to make the most of whatever chance you get. Make yourself as useful and knowledgeable as possible in your area of interest. A consistent theme mentioned by professionals is that if you do good work, you will be remembered for it, and being remembered is essential with regards to networking.

4. **The most important takeaways from high school and parts of college are soft skills rather than industry-specific knowledge.** Professionals consistently reiterated the importance of having strong oral and written communication skills. Almost universally, the ability to explain ideas to the audience at hand was identified as imperative. Particularly, professionals from fields relating to science, technology, engineering, and math made a point to dispel any beliefs that communication skills were less important in their respective fields (especially for those who aspire to reach management positions).

5. **Learn technology!** It is on its way to playing an integral role in all fields. You do not need to be a computer scientist, but just understand that technology can be an enabler, be it for communication, analysis, art, music, or simplifying repetitive tasks so that you can focus on more strategic work. Knowing technology will frequently help you and is unlikely to hurt you.

CPSIA information can be obtained
at www.ICGtesting.com
Printed in the USA
JSHW032232160921
18755JS00004B/5